Nathaniel Hawthorne (July 4, 1804 – May 19, 1864) was an American novelist, dark romantic, and short story writer. His works often focus on history, morality, and religion. He was born in 1804 in Salem, Massachusetts, to Nathaniel Hathorne and the former Elizabeth Clarke Manning. His ancestors include John Hathorne, the only judge involved in the Salem witch trials who never repented of his actions. He entered Bowdoin College in 1821, was elected to Phi Beta Kappa in 1824, and graduated in 1825. He published his first work in 1828, the novel Fanshawe; he later tried to suppress it, feeling that it was not equal to the standard of his later work. He published several short stories in periodicals, which he collected in 1837 as Twice-Told Tales. The next year, he became engaged to Sophia Peabody. He worked at the Boston Custom House and joined Brook Farm, a transcendentalist community, before marrying Peabody in 1842. The couple moved to The Old Manse in Concord, Massachusetts, later moving to Salem, the Berkshires, then to The Wayside in Concord. (Source: Wikipedia)

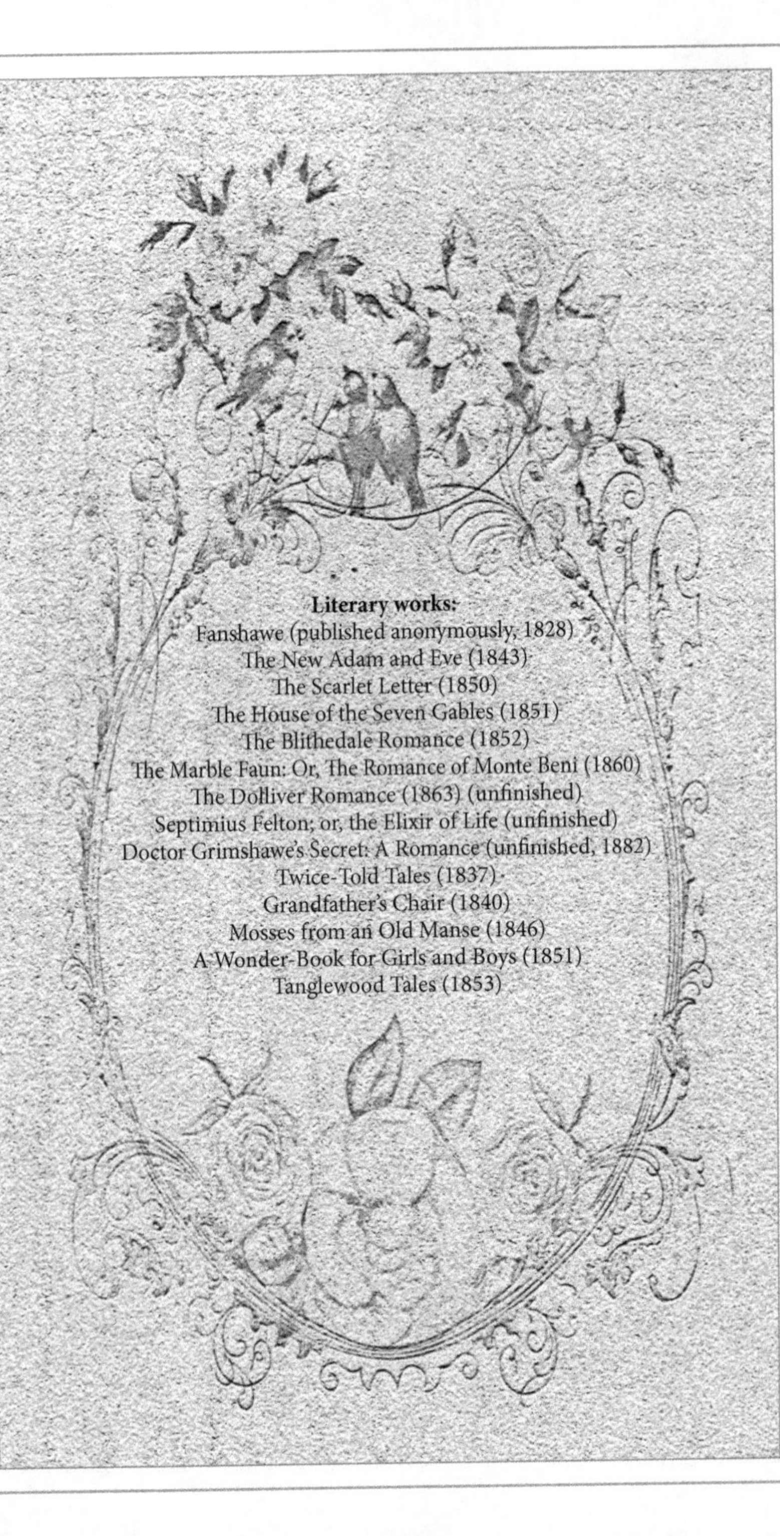

Literary works:

Fanshawe (published anonymously, 1828)
The New Adam and Eve (1843)
The Scarlet Letter (1850)
The House of the Seven Gables (1851)
The Blithedale Romance (1852)
The Marble Faun: Or, The Romance of Monte Beni (1860)
The Dolliver Romance (1863) (unfinished)
Septimius Felton; or, the Elixir of Life (unfinished)
Doctor Grimshawe's Secret: A Romance (unfinished, 1882)
Twice-Told Tales (1837)
Grandfather's Chair (1840)
Mosses from an Old Manse (1846)
A Wonder-Book for Girls and Boys (1851)
Tanglewood Tales (1853)

THE SCARLET STIGMA
A DRAMA IN FOUR ACTS

NATHANIEL HAWTHORNE

PRINCE CLASSICS

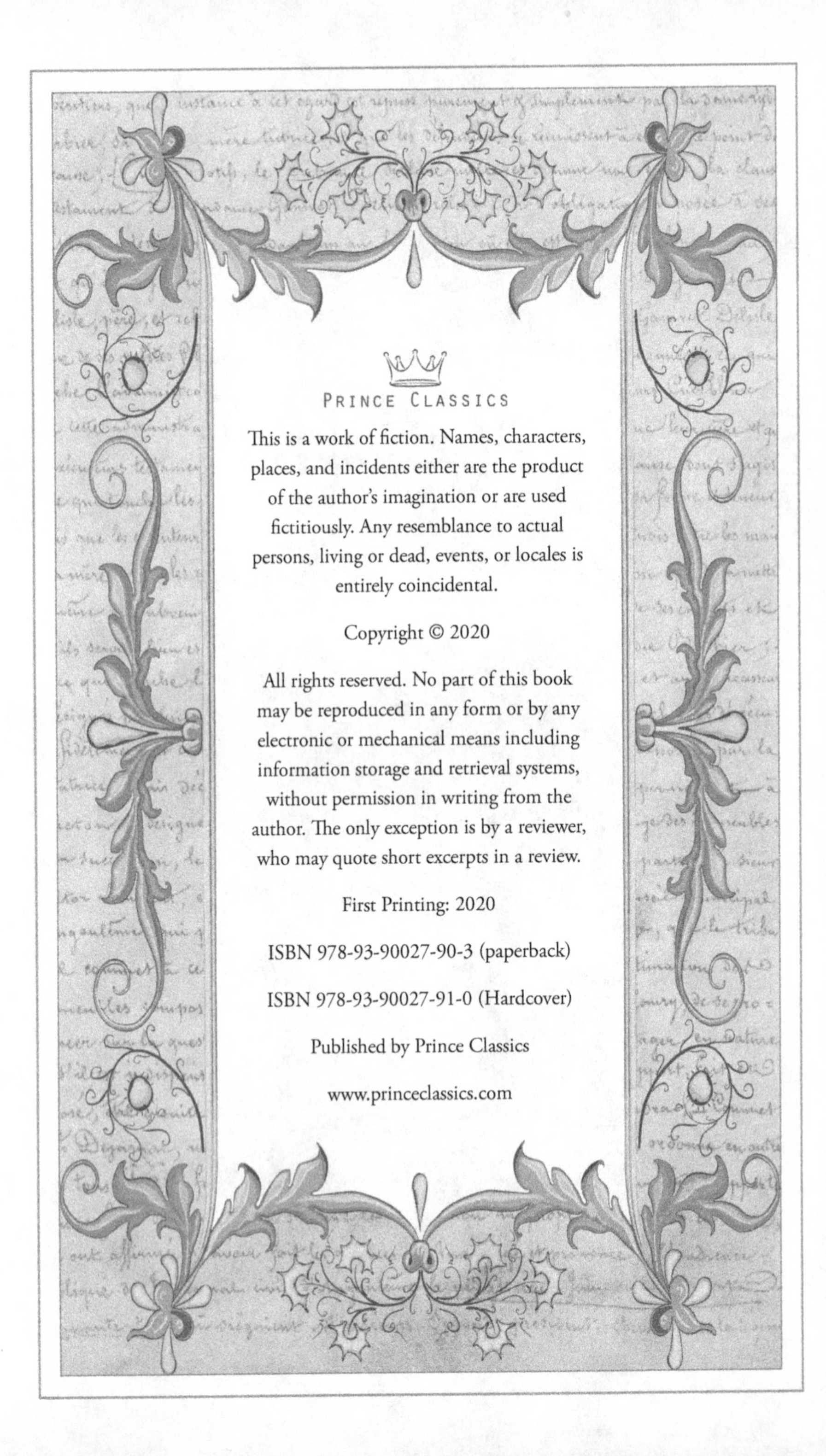

PRINCE CLASSICS

First Printing: 2020

ISBN 978-93-90027-90-3 (paperback)

ISBN 978-93-90027-91-0 (Hardcover)

Published by Prince Classics

www.princeclassics.com

Contents

THE SCARLET STIGMA
A DRAMA IN FOUR ACTS

Founded upon Nathaniel Hawthorne's Novel,

"The Scarlet Letter."

Stigmatization

Stigmatization is a rare incident of ecstasy. Not many well authenticated cases have been reported by competent medical authorities, and yet there can be no doubt of its occasional occurrence. See Encyclopaedia Britannica, article on Stigmatization by Dr. Macalister, and references therein cited; also the work on Nervous and Mental Diseases by Dr. Landon Carter Gray, page 511. That it may occur in men of a high order of ability is instanced by the case of St. Francis of Assisi.

It ought not to be necessary to point out that the entire third scene in the second act of this play is a dramatic transcript from the diseased consciousness of Mr. Dimsdell, that the Satan of the play is an hallucination, and that the impress of the stigma upon Dimsdell's breast is merely the culmination of his auto-hypnotic ecstasy, or trance.

PERSONS REPRESENTED.

ROGER PRYNNE, called *Chillingworth*, a physician.

ARTHUR DIMSDELL, a youthful divine.

JOHN WILSON, a good old minister.

BELLINGHAM, Governor of the Colony.

BUTTS, a sea captain.

SATAN, an hallucination of Dimsdell's.

BRONSON, Members of the Governor's Council.

WARD, Members of the Governor's Council.

LANGDON, Members of the Governor's Council.

ARNOLD, Members of the Governor's Council.

DIGGORY, a servant to Governor Bellingham.

HESTER PRYNNE, wife of Roger Prynne.

MARTHA WILSON, daughter of Rev. John Wilson.

URSULA, a nurse.

BETSEY, a milkmaid.

MOTHER CAREY, keeper of a sailor's inn.

A Clerk, a Crier, a Jailer, Councilors, Citizens, Soldiers, Sailors, Indians, Servants.

SCENE—*Boston.* TIME—*June, 1668.*

Act I.

Scene I.

A tavern and a street in front of it. Settles on porch. SAILORS *smoking and drinking. Enter* CAPTAIN BUTTS, *singing.*

Butts. *The Margery D. was a trim little ship,*
The men they could man, and the skipper could skip;
She sailed from her haven one fine summer day,
And she foundered at sea in the following way,—
To-wit:

All. *A-rinkety, clinkety, clink, clank, clank,*
The liquor they bathed in, the spirits they drank;
A sailor at sea with three sheets in the wind
Can hardly be called, sirs, quite sober.

Enter MOTHER CAREY, *from Tavern.*

Carey. Cap'n! Cap'n Butts! Gen'le gen'lemen! would ye rune a pore widdy woman by a singing of sech filthy tunes? And me up for my license again nex' Tuesday!

Butts. Peace! Peace, Mother Carey, hear your chickens screech! Come, boys!

[*Singing.*

The captain was thirsty, and so was each man,

They ladled the grog out by cup and by can,

The night it was stormy, they knew not the place,

And they sang as they sank the following grace,—

To-wit:

All. *A-sinkety, sinkety, sink, sank, sunk,*

Our captain is tipsy, our mate is quite drunk,

Our widows we leave to the world's tender care

And we don't give a damn for the Devil!

Ha! Ha! Ha!

Carey. O, Lord! O, Lord! If the magistrates should hear that song, they'd close my place!

Butts. There, there now. [*Chucks her under the chin.*] The magistrates are not as quick to hear a sailor sing as thou art to take his orders. Bring us a pint apiece.

Carey. Thou naughty man! [*Slaps his jaws.*] A pint apiece?

[*Exit.*

Butts. Aye. Now, lads, bargain out your time; ye'll not see a petticoat for many a day.

[*Lights pipe and sits.*

Sailors. Aye, aye, sir.

CITIZENS cross stage, singly and in groups, all going in the same direction. Enter MOTHER CAREY *from house with ale, serves it, looks up and down street as in expectation of some one, then goes in.*

Butts. Mother Carey's lost one of her chicks. Here lads! here's to the mousey Puritan lassies! They won't dance, they can't sing—Ah! well! here's to them till we come again!

[*All drink.*

Enter along the street two COUNCILORS.

Arnold. 'Tis very true; but, sir, though many break this law and go unpunished, our godly Company should not wink at known adultery.

Langdon. In other words, we must find scape-goats to bear our sins.

Arnold. Nay, not exactly that. We vindicate God's laws, and——

[*Exeunt Councilors.*

Butts. He must be Privy Councilor to the Lord Himself!

Enter a group of WOMEN.

First Woman. Her beauty, say'st thou? Pretty is as pretty does, say I. I'd beauty her! Go to! Who knows the father of her brat; can any tell?

Second Woman. Thou dost not doubt thy goodman?

First Woman. Trust none of them. I know mine own; dost thou know thine? As for her she hath shamed our sex, and I would—

[*Exeunt Women.*

Butts. God's-my-life, there's more poison in their tongues than in a nest of rattlesnakes? What's all this pother, lads?

Sailor. There's a trial, sir, on a charge of bastardy.

Butts. Ha! ha! ha! You rogues had better ship elsewhere; if the wind sits in that quarter, you'll find foul weather here.

Sailors. Ha! ha! ha!

More people cross the stage.

Butts. Cheapside on a holiday!

Re-enter MOTHER CAREY, *dressed for walking.*

Carey. O, dear! O, dear! I'll be late; I'm sure I'll be late. Oh! dear, dear, dear! why will that Ursula still lag?

Butts. What's the matter, Mother?

Carey. Matter? Matter enough! a gentlewoman tried for adultery and me sure to miss it all! [*Looks around.*] Why doesn't Ursula come? O, dear! O, dear!—why, here she is!

Enter URSULA.

What kept thee, Ursula?

Ursula. Such a crowd! Whew! I'm out o' breath. [*Sits; one or two pass over.*] The town's run mad to look upon a gentlewoman shamed. [*Citizens still pass.*] Ah! there's no room for me now, but when her labor came God knows there was no press! I had room enough then, not one would lend a hand—fie! they are serpents, all of them; they have double tongues to hiss, but ne'er a hand to help.

Carey. Still talking to herself. Here, Ursula, take the keys and wait upon the gentlemen.

[*Hands keys to Ursula and exit up street.*

Ursula. Let the gentlemen wait on me awhile.

Butts. Would you have us die of thirst, Ursula?

Ursula. What will you have, Captain?

Butts. Stingo, Ursula, stingo!

[*Exit Ursula in tavern.*

What say you, lads, shall we see this trial?

Sailor. Aye, aye, sir, the woman's fair to look upon.

Butts. Then let us get our ballast in, hoist sail and tack away.

Re-enter URSULA *with ale.*

Who is it, Ursula, they try?

Ursula. A gentle lady, sir. God's-my-life, had no man tempted her—but, that's your ways, you tempt us, blame us when we yield, and then make laws to punish us.

Butts. But, what's her name?

Ursula. What should it be but Hester Prynne?

Butts. Hester Prynne? The gentle Mistress Prynne I brought from Amsterdam three years ago?

Ursula. The same, God bless her.

Butts. My lads, don't wait for me.

[*Exeunt Sailors.*

I knew her husband, Ursula; a man

Well versed in all the wisdom of the time;

Somewhat well gone in years, but lovable

Beyond the shallowness of youth, and rich

In mellow charity. Oft hath he sailed

With me from port to port where learning drew him,

And still came richer home. One day he shipped

For Amsterdam and brought his bride, who, like

A hawthorn in its pink of youth that blushes

'Neath the shadow of an ancient elm,

Shed spring-time sweetness round his green old age.

I've seen them often in their Holland home,

Where wisdom laid its treasures at the feet

Of love, and beauty crowned the offering.

She was a lovely lady, Ursula,

And when her lord, still bent on learning more,

Resolved to come out to America—

His own affairs then calling him to England—

He placed her in my care, intending soon

To follow her. He did, but curséd fate!

His ship was lost—no one knows where!

Ursula. Alack

The day! She had not sinned had he been here.

Butts. But, didst thou know her, Ursula, as I

Have known her, wisely good and true, thou wouldst

Have wondered more.

Ursula. Know her, sir! I nursed her!

Butts. Thou, Ursula?

Ursula. None but I!

Butts. Where were her friends?

Ursula. Where, but at home! Dear heart,

They shunned her like the plague—though if the truth

Were known, many that shun her now would keep

Her company perforce. None came near

But pious Master Dimsdell, and even he

Came only out of duty to her soul;

He told me so.

Butts. The Reverend Master Dimsdell

And thou her only comforters?

Ursula. Nay,

The little bairn was her greatest comfort, sir.

Butts. How doth she bear her trouble, Ursula?

Ursula. Like a good woman, sir.

Butts. She yet is that!

But have you never learned her lover's name?

Ursula. Nay, I never have.

Butts. 'Tis strange that she

Should fall; and then endeavor to conceal

Her lover! Noble, wise and beautiful,

No other than a man of mark could win her!

Ursula. A three years widow, baby three months old,

A coward run-a-gate of a lover, sir—

Tell me, is there no exception made

By law for widows?

Butts. None, of which I know.

Ursula. The law is hard indeed!

Butts. I wonder if

A rough sea-dog like me might speak a word

For her?

Ursula. Aye, that you might! Go seek the good

Old Doctor Wilson, mercy dwells with him,

And he will aid you, sir.

Butts. I'll go at once.

[*Exeunt severally, Butts up street, Ursula in tavern.*

Enter Roger Prynne, *travel stained.*

Roger. We are not masters of our paths, although

Our wills do seem to guide our faltering steps:

Ship voyagers are we, and roam at will

Within the narrow confines of the deck,

But neither plot nor steer the destined course.

I may have passed her house—I'll ask my way

Here at the inn. Long live King Boniface!

What ho! some wine!

Ursula. [*Within*] Your patience, Captain, I'll be there anon.

Roger. At your leisure, hostess; I've learned to wait.

[*Sits.*

A bachelor at sixty, I found myself

Encumbered with a ward—nay, not that—

Enriched with female loveliness and grace

Bequeathed unto me by a dying friend.

Volition had no part in that, nor in

My sudden recrudescency of love.

I willed our marriage; but 'twas fate bestowed

The joys I long had fled. Then came our life

In Amsterdam; each day so filled with bliss

It overflowed into the next, and days

Of joy grew into weeks and months of happiness—

Let me have wine, I say!

Ursula. [*Within*] Coming, sir!

Roger. Anon the traveling itch—was't fate or will—

Possessed my soul to see America,

And money matters calling me to London,

Where raged the plague, I sent my wife before me

To America with Captain Butts, then bound

For Boston. Ah! well-a-day, the parting!—

I hurried up my business; fled London town;

Shipped for America; was wrecked far South;

Captured by Indians; escaping, wandered North

Until I found the white man's colonies;

And now footsore and old I've reached the place

I first intended. What next, O, Fate?

Enter URSULA.

Good morrow, hostess.

Ursula. Good morrow, sir.

[*Surprised.*

Roger. Look not

Askance upon my way-worn clothes; there's gold

To pay my reckoning.

[*Throwing money down.*

Ursula. Your pardon, sir;

I marveled, sir, so fine a gentleman

Should be so travel-stained. What will you have?

Roger. Bring me a cup of sherris-sack.

Ursula. [*Aside*] I knew he was a gentleman!

[*Exit.*

Roger. How will my Hester greet me? Will she know me?

She never saw me with a beard, nor in

Such rags. Perhaps she thinks me dead—

If so, the shock might kill her—Let me see—

Putative widows have before my time

Bought second husbands with their beauty, wealth,

Or wit—and she hath all. 'Tis probable—

And when the long-supposed defunct returned,

He found his amorous relict the bride

Of a bright-eyed youth! What worse, ye harpy fates?

She may be dead! Oh! this is madness!

Sweet Heaven, let her live! and, if I find

Her married, I'll depart unknown to her

And bury in my heart's deep sepulchre

My widowed grief. Bah! I'm a fool!

This weakness comes from my long wandering!

Misfortunes, though we think we conquer them,

Ever pursue, hang on our rear, and give

Such rankling wounds as teach our souls to dread

What else may lie in wait invincible.

Re-enter URSULA *with wine.*

Ursula. I beg your pardon, sir. I could not find the wine at first.

Roger. Why, how was that?

Ursula. I'm not the hostess, sir, she is away; I merely take her place till she comes back.

Roger. You fill it rarely.

Ursula. God bless thee, sir, I'm cook, nurse, or hostess, as people need me. Ursula Cook, Ursula Nurse, or Ursula Goodale, at your service, sir.

Roger. Ah, indeed, Ursula! Then I presume thou knowest many of the citizens?

Ursula. I know them everyone.

Roger. This wine is excellent. [*Drinking*] Dost know one Roger Prynne?

Ursula. The husband of our Hester Prynne?

Roger. The same. [*Aside*] Thank God, she lives.

Ursula. He's dead, sir, rest his soul, a more than thirty months ago.

Roger. Poor fellow! He was a friend of mine. Where did they bury him?

Ursula. His ship was wrecked, he had no burial.

Roger. Here's to his memory! You know his wife?

Ursula. Alas; I do, sweet lady!

Roger. And why alas? The loss of a husband is no great calamity in a colony. There can be no dearth here of husband-material, I fancy.

Ursula. Whence come you that you know so little of the doings here?

Roger. From the far South, where for two long years and more I've lived among the savages. What do you mean?

Ursula. I mean her trial by the magistrates.

Roger. Tried by magistrates? For what?

Ursula. Adultery.

Roger. Tried for adultery?

Ursula. Aye, sir, that she is.

Roger. It is a lie, a damned lie! Tried for adultery! A likely thing! So pure a woman! A purer creature never lived!

Ursula. Sir, you are her friend? You know her?

Roger. I am—I am her husband—her husband's friend. I knew her in Old England. Adultery! A pretty word! Who doth accuse her? Damned detractors!

Ursula. Her child.

Roger. Her what?

Ursula. Her child.

Roger. Hath Hester Prynne a child? Well, well; that is news indeed! God bless the little thing! it can't be quite as much as three years old; nay, not so old. Why, such a tot can give no testimony. I'll go to this trial; I may be able yet to aid her. Adultery! Bah!

Ursula. God bless your heart, sir.

Roger. Is't a boy or girl, how old?

Ursula. A girl and three months old.

Roger. Three months? Three years you mean.

Ursula. Three months, I said.

Roger. Thou dost not mean that Hester Prynne hath borne a child within the last two years?

Ursula. I do. [*Aside*] A strange man, truly. This news hath troubled him; but that's not strange, it troubles all her friends. He seemed glad enough she had a child, but when I said it was a girl it seemed to sting him. Well, well! God help the women; we are unwelcome when we come, abused while we stay, and driven hence with ill-usage.

Roger. Adulteress! That cannot be! There's some

Mistake, or some deceit in this. Her great

Nobility of heart would take upon

Herself another's wrong. I'll take an oath

The babe they say is hers she never bore!

Ursula. 'Tis surely hers, for I delivered her.

Roger. Hester! Hester! O, my God! My Hester!

Woman, didst thou say that she is married?

Ursula. Nay, I said she is a widow, sir.

Roger. Who is her paramour?

Ursula. I do not know.

[*Busies herself removing tankards.*

Roger. [*Aside*] Now is my honored name dragged in the dust

By her to whom I did confide its keeping;

And she herself, my cherished wife, upraised

Upon a pedestal of shameful guilt

For filthy mouths to spit their venom at.

Slowly now. Whatever haps I'll be

Cornelius Tacitus for the nonce, nor brave

My state with that true name which marks me out

As Publius Cornutus. I must have time to think.

[*To Ursula*] Get me more wine. Prepare a room for me.

Ursula. Aye, sir. [*Going.*]

Roger. Where is this trial held?

Ursula. Sir, at the Market place, three crossings up

The street and to the left.

Roger. I thank thee. Go.

[*Exit Ursula.*

Why was the banishment of tyrant fate

Annulled by vigorous will? and why should I,

For whom the jaws of death unhinged themselves,

Escape from shipwreck, war, and pestilence,

And here attain my journey's end at last,

But that such evil deaths were much too mild

To gratify the fury that pursues me!

I was reserved for this last ignominy

As in despite of human purposes;

Robbed of mine honor where most I placed my trust

And reap this pain where most I sowed for peace.

Was it for this that I did marry her?

Was it for this I sent her here before me?

For this I nursed the holy purposes

Of wedded purity, o'ercame the shocks

Of human destiny, and held in check

The inward passions of the baser man?

For this—to be cornuted in mine age

And die a by-word?

My purposes! My purposes! O, God!

Our purposes are little nine-pins

Which fate's sure aim bowls down incessantly:

As fast as we can set them up, events

Roll down the narrow alleys of our lives,

Rumbling like distant thunder as they speed,

Till crash! our king-intent is down, and in

His fall share all his puny retinue!

She an adulteress! My Hester, whom

I cherished as my soul! How I loved her!

Forgotten, like the meat of yesterday,

Let it pass!

Henceforth, for me there's nothing on this side

Of Hell, but study of revenge on him

Who wrought her shame. He must have used foul means;

For she was ever chaste in thought and deed.

Hell fiend! Now, under an assuméd name,

I'll ferret out her lusty paramour;

Contrive some means to deeply punish him,

And satisfy my fathomless revenge.

[*Exit.*

Scene II.

Another street. Enter Rev. Arthur Dimsdell, *alone.*

Dimsdell. 'Twould do no good.—The Governor is late,

Or I have missed him.—Confess?—Disgrace for me;

No help to her; and all the blasphemies

That evil minds could cast on sacred calling

Would be my blame. Whereas, I now can make

My pleas take on the color of mine office

And yet reflect on it a purer glow.—

Why comes he not?—The path of righteousness,

Though straight, leads on thro' pleasant fields to Heaven,

Whereas the broad and easy road of sin

Splits in its downward way, and then the will

Stands at a halt which fork to take, though both

Lead on to Hell! Now—why, here he comes!

Enter Governor*, attended.*

Governor. Nay, Dimsdell, plead no more; she must be tried.

I know what thou wouldst say, and like thee for it;

But think, my friend, the law would mock itself

If pardon did precede the penalty.

Dimsdell. Our Lord did pardon one was taken in

The very act. O, think of Him!

Governor. Enough!

What! wouldst thou have our laws contemned

As feeble nets to catch the smaller fry

And let the great break through? I tell thee, sir,

Her wealth, her beauty, her hitherto fair fame,

Blacken her crime and make its punishment

A signal warning to the baser sort.

Dimsdell. Hath she not suffered pains and imprisonment?

Enough to answer all the decalogue?

Governor. I stand for law; and you, I think, do think

You stand for gospel.—Come, we tarry.—

Plead with the Council for the woman, and, while

I think her death were well deserved, I'll not

Oppose their mercy if you win it.

My hand upon it.

[*Going.*

Dimsdell. If that she be condemned,

Suspend her sentence till her paramour

Be found; and let them die together.

Governor. Agreed. Come, we're late.

[*Exeunt.*

Scene III.

The Market Place.—Church with Portico, L.—A pillory on a raised Platform, R.—The Governor *and* Council *seated in portico.—A crowd of* TOWNSFOLK.

Governor. Now that our other business is dispatched,

Call Hester Prynne.

Wilson. Wise Governor, and you,

My brethren: dried as I am with age,

The tendrils of my heart are pliable;

Nor have the tangles of this thicket-world

So twisted all my grain as not to bend

Before another's misery. Wherefore,

I do beseech you, call her not.

Governor. Yet must

We try the woman, though we pity her;

And though the scion mercy grafts upon

The stock of justice, the stock is justice still.

Wilson. I plead for justice! even-handed justice!

As blind and cold as death—but with a sword,

Sharp on one side to reach the woman's heart

And on the other keener for the man's!

You call the woman; where's her paramour?

Governor. We do not know.

Wilson. Then grant a stay to Hester

Till he's known.

Governor. Too late; nor were it good

To let the woman slap the face of law,

And not resent it quickly. Once again,

Call Hester Prynne. The man she may discover.

Enter REV. ARTHUR DIMSDELL *through crowd and goes to Portico.*

Crier. Hester Prynne! Hester Prynne!

[*Exit.*

Dimsdell. Most worthy Governor, I am like one

Who waking hears the village clock toll time,

Yet, having missed the first few strokes, the hour

He cannot tell: and so stand I and hear

Fair Hester called. Is it for trial, or

For punishment?

Governor. For both.

Dimsdell. I am her pastor and I speak for her;

I would to God that I could plead "Not guilty,"

Or in her stead could offer up myself

To satisfy the law!

Crowd. How good he is!

Dimsdell. Gentle and wise she is, grave councilors,

And with a modest meekness goes about

The daily duties of her household care;

Oh! I am sure no vulgar palate-bait

Did lure her to this shame, but some enticement

That took the form of higher nature did

Invest the hook. For she is modesty

Itself.

Governor. Can modesty, then, fall like this?

Dimsdell. The modesty of woman is like the blush
Upon a tender rose; it is her treasure
And her ornament: you cannot touch it,
But it fades away; or breathe upon it,
But it loses perfume; or bring it to the light,
Unwilted.

Governor. True, but when the roses fade
We cast them forth, nor treasure them again.

Dimsdell. 'Tis thus I own; but we have higher teaching.
Our Lord, who knew temptation's mighty power,
Yet was himself without sin's damning stain,
Did pass upon a case like this. "Let him
Who hath no sin first cast a stone at her."
And then He said, "Go, woman, sin no more."
Oh! wondrous grace that pardoned frailty
Which had not sunk to vice!

Re-enter CRIER with HESTER PRYNNE.

Governor. Enough! Here comes the woman.
Hester, thou art accused before this court
Of that which blushing virtue shrinks to name,
Adultery.

Hester. I pray you spare me.

Governor. Thou art the widow of a man of whom

Report spake only praise: no act of thine

Hath openly offended decency,

But that young life which draws its sustenance

From thy round breast avows thy hidden shame.

Hester. Have mercy on the babe, O, God!

Governor. That thou shouldst sin, and thereby, Hester, bring

Dishonor on the name thy spouse did give thee,

Is worse than in a meaner woman. If thou

Hast aught to say to mitigate the wrath

Of justice, speak. And, Hester, bear in mind

The penalty is death or banishment.

Hester. I would not gloze my crime, nor do I know

How to address your worships.

Yet since you bid me I will plead my cause

As best I can.

That I have sinned is true; and well I know

Henceforth for me there's nothing left from all

My kind but scorn and hate.

For me hath life no charm to cheat my hope,

Or make me wish to linger here; yet I

While lives the child would shelter her, the one

Sweet flower that lovely grows above the soil

Of my most foul debasement.

Although the blossom of iniquity,

She takes no tinct from whence she springs, but rather

Of the sky toward which she doth unfold.

Believe me, sirs,

But for my babe's dear love, I'd ask for death

To rid me quickly of my misery:

For love itself, dishonored in my being,

Turns all the gentle cords that bind affection

Into hard-knotted thongs to whip me hence.

Therefore, if I do plead for life, think not

I do beseech a favor for myself,

But rather, that I beg a lingering pain,

Than expiate in one quick-ending pang

The sum of all my loathéd wickedness.

Thus, for my tender babe, I ask my life,

And, for myself, I do implore you now,

Banish me not.

As for my crime, I have repented it

Most bitterly; yea, I've suffered anguish

From the very hour when, as the spring

Of nature dragged my anchors loose, the soft

Entreaty of a lover's sigh did blow

Concurrent with my tide, and swept me out

Into a troubled sea.

Now, battered on the rocks of hard opinions,

My most untimely wreck is quite complete;

Yet spare the hulk for that dear freight it bore.

Governor. Woman, I pity thee; now, while our laws

Are strict, yet may our mercy show itself

In staving off the penalty, if thou

Wilt aid us.

Hester. Your mercy comes with hard condition;

For how can I, who stand here helpless,

Aid you who have all power?

Governor. Tell us who is thy paramour?

Hester. That I will not do.

Governor. Thou art most obstinate. What say you now,

Grave councilors? Need we delay the sentence?

Bronson. Quick to forgive and slow in condemnation,

Would be our wisest course in such a case.

The life she hath God gave; we should not take it;

Nor should we banish her, for she is useful,

And with her needle doth assist the poor.

There is provision in our law to fit

This crime when neither death nor banishment

Is proper. It is: [*Reading*] "Th' adulteress shall stand

Upon the pillory; and on her breast

Shall wear a scarlet letter A, to mark

Her criminal incontinence."

Governor. A good

Suggestion truly; we had forgot the clause

From long disuse. What say you?

Ward. I think it wise.

Arnold. 'Twill be more merciful.

Langdon. A living warning 'gainst adultery.

All. It is our suffrage.

Governor. So be it then.

Hester, thou art to stand upon the pillory

A little while, and wear upon thy breast

The Scarlet Letter "A" forever;

This see thou do on pain of instant death

Or banishment. Hath anyone a piece

Of scarlet cloth?

Bronson. I have the letter here prepared.

Governor. Clerk, affix the letter to her breast.

Enter Roger Prynne, *clad as in Scene I.—He keeps to the rear of Hester.*

Now, Jailer, lead her to the pillory,

There let her stand unbound.

Hester ascends steps to pillory platform.

Dimsdell, you are her pastor, speak to her.

Hold up her sin before her eyes, and warn

The multitude by her example.

Dimsdell. I beg you, sir, let Dr. Wilson speak.

Wilson. Nay, Dimsdell. Nay, the charge is yours.

Speak on. And plead that she disclose the man

Who was her paramour.

Dimsdell. I pray you pardon me. I am not well.

Governor. Not well? 'Tis but compassion weakens thee.

Speak man! thy words are gentlest and will draw

Her secret from her, though ours do seal her lips.

Proceed, Dimsdell.

Dimsdell. We wrong her nature when we seek to know

That which her heart doth teach her to conceal;

Yet at your bidding will I plead with her.

Goes over to pillory.

Hester, look down upon me; let thine ear

Receive my meaning with the sound I make;

Behold in me the body of the Council,

Not me alone; and hear my words as though

The general voice, speaking in concert true,

Did intone them.

For it were vain presumption to expect

That, what the Governor could not extract,

My words alone could move thee to disclose.

Roger. A modest gentleman, truly!

Dimsdell. Upon thy sin I dwell not; the penalty

Which thou dost suffer preaches repentance;

And in thy nature there is naught to lead thee

Twice astray.

There's not an eye that now doth look upon thee

But pities thee, and doubt thou not, if he

Who wronged thee is present here, his heart is wrung

With bitterest remorse. Wilt speak his name?

Hester. I will not.

Dimsdell. I do command thee by the Commonwealth,

I do entreat thee for thy reputation,

I do implore thee for thy soul's salvation,

Give up his name.

Hester. I would not breathe his name to anyone;

Nay, not to him who was my husband, though

The sea should cast him up to question me.

Roger. Woman, who did seduce thee?

Hester. I keep my vow.

Dimsdell. Hester, deceive thyself no more; look down

Upon me once again. Believe me, Hester,

No pain the world could now inflict would harm

Thy recreant lover. To see thee here set up

The target of a thousand curious eyes,

Thy beauties blistered in the noonday sun,

Thy gentle breast seared with yon scarlet letter,

Would burn that image on his soul. Have mercy,

Hester, forgive his cowardice, do thou

Act for him; pronounce his name and let him die

To satisfy his crime.

Hester. I will not drag him down with me.

Roger. Oh! glorious generosity misplaced!

Dimsdell. Your generosity hath led you once

Astray; do not allow it now to aid

Him in hypocrisy. For, Hester, you,

Who know his weaknesses and aspirations,

His station in his calling, his place in life

Among us, will be a party to deception

If now you hide his name.

Hester. I answer to my God. No man shall know

That which is only known to me and him.

But speak thou on his crime!

Dimsdell. Ho! all ye people of the commonwealth!

Behold!—let him confess!—O, Hester! speak!—

I see—no more—

[*Dimsdell falls.*

Throng, confused and amazed, closes around Dimsdell.

Cries of horror and apprehension.

Governor. Look to our brother Dimsdell. He faints;

The heat hath overcome him.

Roger. I am a doctor. Make room!

The falling sickness. Give us breathing space!

Governor. Hester, thou art discharged. Let all go home!

[*Exeunt.*

Act II.

Scene I.

Interior of Hester's home. Furniture Dutch-English, comfortable and handsome. Windows draped in scarlet-fringed curtains with scarlet cross-cords, simulating the letter "A." Rich needle work in the hangings and other accessories. A cradle L., near it a table with a quarto Bible. Hester *discovered bending over cradle, then sits R.C. and takes up a piece of embroidery (the letter "A" in scarlet on a dark background).*

Hester. God bless the little darling, how she sleeps!

Had I but thought that all my heart would beat

Within the tender compass of her arms,

I had not prayed she might not be. But now,

Although unasked she came, unasked she brought

A wealth of love and blessing to my soul.

[*Sits and embroiders.*]

Thus Providence, although it pierce the heart,

Works into it some glorious design;

Which on this under side of life is blurred,

Thread over thread in infinite confusion.

Or, if we are not made of firmest texture,

The work pulls through, or tears an ugly rent,

Or gathers up our woof in meshy tangles.

This is a world of worn and fretted ends,

Knit in a maze of fearful intricacy,

Wherein we see no meaning. Nor can we know

The hidden shuttles of Eternity,

That weave the endless web of living, loving,

And begetting, whereby a filament

Of earth takes on the likeness of an angel.

The primal burden of our race-existence,

Mankind's perpetual perpetuation,

Weighs on weak womanhood; we bear the race

And all its natural ills, yet still our fellows,

Who proudly call themselves our lords and masters,

Do heap upon us petty wrongs, and load

Us down with their oppressions. I cannot tell

What rich reward my suffering may bring,

But bide the piercing, like this patient cloth,

In hope the needle carries golden thread.

Enter a Maid-Servant.

What is it?

Servant. Madam, a gentleman would speak with you.

Hester. Bid him enter.

[*Exit Servant.*

Methought I heard my husband's dreaded voice

Speak to me on the pillory. What

If he lives, or hath arisen from the dead

To reckon with me now? Well, let him come;

For this strong heart outcast from sympathy

Hath turned back on itself in double strength;

And all the puny woman of my mind,

Burned in the furnace of my sex's scorn,

Plunged in the icy vat of love's neglect,

Hath tempered hard. I fear him not.

Enter ROGER PRYNNE, *shaved, and dressed as a doctor of medicine.*

Roger himself!

Roger. Thou didst provide snug quarters, Hester, against my coming. Aye, and hast furnished them better than I bade thee.

Hester. The cost was small; my needle and my energy—

Roger. Have done the work; yea, and supplied the cradle also. Ah! 'tis a brave piece of work; very beautiful and delicate; the lusty offspring of lustful parents. Somewhat costly, I should think, and asked some pains. Methinks, thou hadst some help with that; or was it thy needle or thy energy which wrought this dainty bit?

Hester. Touch not the child; 'tis mine, thou hast no part in it.

Roger. Too true. But calm thyself. I have not harmed the brat, nor did I touch it. [*Looking around.*] I like thy taste, Hester. A handsome house to hold a handsome woman.

Hester. The house is thine; let me and my babe depart.

Roger. Nay, keep the house, 'twill shelter you; I do not need it.

Hester. I will not have it.

Roger. Will not, Madam Hester, is a strong word to use to your wedded lord and master. I say you shall; yea, and, furthermore, here is provision for the child and thee.

[*Throwing purse upon the table.*]

Hester. Take up thy purse. I who have done thee wrong will not henceforth eat thy bread.

Roger. Wrong, Hester. Done me wrong? Wronged me? Nay, Hester, wronged thyself; wronged thine innocent babe; wronged the world; wronged whom thou wilt, but not wronged me! To wake me from a doting dream—that was not wrong! A dream of woman's purity and innocence; a foolish dream of married happiness between thy youth and my decrepitude; to put an end to such a madness, surely was not wrong! Wronged me? Thy levity hath righted my poor mind, which, pondering o'er thy beauties, listed to one side.

Hester. Oh! pardon me!

Roger. Pardon thee? yea, why should I not? I do pardon thee; yea, more, I do applaud thine act. Thou wast no slothful servant; thou didst not fear the coming of thy lord; thou puttest all to use and gottest cent per cent. Therefore, the care I show for thee is hire and wages; it is thy due, accept it freely.

Hester. Let me and my babe depart. Receive thy money and thy house, I can take nothing from thee. Ah! if I could I would return thee every penny I have spent of thine.

Roger. Wait till I ask thee to account. What! am I so old, and yet not know the cost of dalliance? Nothing dearer. And he who eared my field during my absence, being now, in thy abasement, so chary of his presence, spent little of his gold, I'll warrant. Who is he, Hester?

Hester. Thou shalt never know.

Roger. Never's a long word, Hester; it stretches beyond the judgment into eternity. Come, I'll know him then, tell me now.

Hester. He is a scholar and can cope with thee; thou canst not find him.

Roger. If he do walk the earth, I'll find him out; if he be now in Hell, I'll follow him; where'er he be, his peace is forfeited and I will—

Hester. What wilt thou do to him?

Roger. Nothing, Hester, nothing. I merely wish to thank him for the love he showed thee during my absence, whereby thou didst mourn for me the less.

Hester. Thou wilt not kill him?

Roger. What a silly thing thou hast become, now thou hast left the path of virtue! Do I kill thee? Am I dangerous? Is there force in this withered body to harm a lusty knave, a brave seducer of ripe womanhood?

Hester. Nay, do not harm him.

Roger. At thy request, mistress.

Hester. The fault was mine.

Roger. No doubt 'twas thine alone.

Hester. Wreak vengeance then on me alone.

Roger. I have none.

Hester. I would I could believe thee.

Roger. As well give faith to me as him. But, truly, Hester, I had thought these puritans, these pilgrim fathers, had left all fleshly lusts behind them with their vanities in England. He must be a rare bird in these parts—O, I shall know him by his plumage!

Hester. He's safe enough.

Roger. Perhaps, but then these poachers, who fish in others' ponds, are proud of their achievements. They will talk. They brag in their cups and strut and ogle when they're sober.

Hester. I'll warn him of thee.

Roger. Thou wilt do nothing of the kind. But come, Hester, man and wife ought not to quarrel. Let us set a good example to the world in peace if not in chastity. Sit you here and listen to me.

Hester. Well?

Roger. Hester, I loved thee when thou wast a babe,

A prattling child no taller than my knee,

A pretty little innocent, a tot

That wavered in its walk and won my heart

By tender trustfulness. Thou'dt leave thy father,

Mother, all, to nestle in these arms

The whiles I told some worn out fairy tale,

Or sang of Robin Hood.

That was before thy mind did take its shape,

And subsequent events have blotted out

All memories of thy babyhood.

Hester. Nay, but I do recall, as in a haze,

Some of the incidents of infancy.

Roger. Perhaps. Hester, thou wast the dearest child

That ever blest fond parents, unfolding sweet

Thy mother's beauties and thy father's strength.

And canst thou now remember who made himself

A child to play with thee vain, foolish games;

Who taught thee out of books such lessons as

Thy little mind could grasp?

Hester. It was thou.

Roger. Then, as thou didst grow toward womanhood,

Some fifteen springs, thy gentle mother died;

A woman beautiful and pure, as sweetly

Ignorant of all her charms as is

The hyacinth.

Hester. Mother! Mother!

Roger. Pray God the saints see nothing here on earth:

Or else that in their golden paradise

Some sleepy potion dull their sympathies

With us: for who could look upon this world,

And see mankind divested of the lies

That make our comeliness; or, with an eye undimmed,

Behold the brutal tragedies of life;

And yet find happiness or peace in Heaven?

Hell's flames would reach unto the tree of life

Itself and singe thy mother's heart, if she

Could see that scarlet letter on thy breast.

[*Hester covers her face and moans.*]

Great God! what thread of continuity

Doth string the whirling incidents of life?

This woman was that maid whose purity

Excelled imagination's greatest reach;

Whose happiness sang ever like the lark

Arising from the earth to soar in Heaven!

And now behold her dyed in scarlet sin,

Branded with infamy, and moaning here

In deepest anguish!

Nay, come; let out thy grief in linkéd words,

For this tooth-gated dumb remorse will herd

Thy thoughts until they gore each other.

Hester, thy strength is greater than to yield

Thus to thy misery; do not lash

Thy heart into a fury; never blow

The tiny sparks of pain

Into the flaming coals of Hell.

That sinning soul is traitor to itself

That leagues its bruiséd thoughts with imps of Hell

To torture conscience.

Hester. Leave me, I pray you.

Roger. Not yet, else were my visit bootless.

Hester, I will not dwell upon thy life

From year to year, nor drag thy colliered soul

Back to its days of spotless innocence.

Thy father's amity for me, thou knowest,

And how, upon his death, I stood toward thee

In place of parents.

Hester. Would you had remained a father to me!

Roger. I loved thee, Hester; daughter, sister, sweetheart,

You were to me. And you did love me too,

And as an elder brother looked on me

In gentle confidence.

So did the years post by in th' dim afterglow

That comes to agéd men; while love with thee
Was in the dawning; a tender sky with both
Of us, my sun already set; and thine
Not yet arisen; nor did it ever rise
To shine on me, fool that I was!

Hester. I never loved you, should not have married you;
Knew nothing then of love except the name.

Roger. Aye, you loved me, and you loved me not;
Hester, I wronged thee when I married thee;
The fault was mine, old as I was, to hope
To still the sweet necessities of youth
With passionless love; nature demands her due,
And we should know, while love may grow at home,
Passion requires some novelty.

Hester. We both have done foul wrong unto each other,
And, as this world doth judge, mine is the greater.

Roger. Yet thou wast tempted by thy youth, my absence,
A handsome lover's importunity:
But what can be said for me, old as I was,
To drive and badger thy chaste ignorance
To marry mine infirmities?

Hester. How can I right this wrong?

Roger. And wouldst thou if thou couldst?

Hester. Aye, if I could; but yet these broken lives,

Cracked by my fall, no putty will make whole.

Roger. Yet canst thou veil my ruin, and o'er me hang

The drapery of silence. Dost consent?

Hester. Aye, but how?

Roger. But swear to me thou wilt conceal my name,

Nor ever claim relationship with me,

Until I bid thee.

Hester. Wherefore the vow?

Roger. Because I wish it;

Perhaps, because I would not bear the scorn,

The petty taunts, the contumelious looks,

That ever greet the cuckold husband.

Hester. Then will I take the oath.

Roger. Swear by the book, and also by the babe,

Never to breathe my rightful name;

Never to claim me as thy husband;

Never to leave this place.

Hester. Wherefore not leave the place?

Roger. Swear, woman, swear!

Never to leave this place, until I bid thee.

Hester. I swear to all these things.

Roger. Swear once again; never to tell thy paramour

Thy husband lives and walks these streets.

Hester. I swear to keep thy counsel as I have kept

His and mine own.

Roger. Remember then, from this time on, my name

Is Chillingworth, no longer Prynne, for that

I will not bear. [*Going*] Hester, farewell.

Yet ere I go, Hester, behold my mind:

I love thee still; but with a chastened heart

Made wise by sorrow. Day after day, as thou

Dost wend thy way about this mazy world,

My care will shield thee and thy little babe.

Do not repulse it. I have no hope that thou

Wilt think of me without revulsion;

Then hate me if thou must; but spare the thought

That ever thou didst take my hateful kisses,

Or clasp those soft warm arms about my thin,

Cold carcass.

Do not despise thy beauties that I once

Did own them. Forget it, Hester, for such a marriage

Was my infamy, and I it was

Who sinned against thy youth. Farewell!

[*Exit.*

Scene II.

A Churchyard. A bell ringing for service. Groups of people standing about. Persons cross stage and enter church door on extreme L.

Bronson. They say the Reverend Master Dimsdell hath

Recovered from his fainting fit, and will,

God willing, preach to us this afternoon.

Langdon. Aye, that he will.

Arnold. But hath he come?

Ward. Not yet;

He's late, but, whether here or elsewhere,

He's always doing good.

Bronson. A kindly man!

His feet do tread th' o'ergrown path that leads

Unto the poor man's door.

Langdon. Aye, that they do!

And, in the darkened hour of mortal grief,

His presence like a lamp gives light and hope.

Arnold. His charity exceeds all human bounds,

And, though he's blameless in himself, knows how

To pardon others.

Ward. Aye, that he doth! Didst note

His plea for Hester Prynne upon her trial?

Langdon. Aye, that I did!

Ward. But know the goodness of it!

He was her constant friend up to the time

Her wantonness declared itself, and then

He left her lonely, as though that punishment

Were all a man of mercy could inflict.

Arnold. He takes it much to heart that wanton vice

Hath found a nest within his congregation.

Langdon. That grief is truly great with him; but yet

He will not hear a word against her.—Look!

For here she comes.

How bravely doth she wear her scarlet letter!

Enter HESTER PRYNNE *alone; walks proudly, with slow steps, to porch and enters church; looking neither to the right nor to the left, but straight before her, with her head up. People turn to look at her, but no one speaks.*

First Woman. The brazen thing!

Second Woman. Didst note the fashion of her badge of vice,

And how she's turned it into ornament?

Third Woman. A handy woman with her needle.

First Woman. Let's in and stare her out of countenance.

[*Exeunt Women.*

Enter Governor Bellingham *and* Roger Prynne, *called Doctor Chillingworth.*

Governor. Now, as I told you, there hath lately come,

But how I know not, a change in him so rare,

It baffles cure.

Roger. I think you said he is

A very studious man?

Governor. Aye, that he is.

Good evening, gentlemen.

All. Your worship.

Roger. I pray you, tell me more.

Governor. Nay, use your eyes,

For here he is.

Enter Rev. Arthur Dimsdell. *People uncover as he passes. He salutes them gravely and generally.*

Dimsdell, a word with you.

Dimsdell. Good evening, gentlemen.

Governor. Dimsdell, here is good Doctor Chillingworth,

Who tended thee. I hope you gentlemen

Will prize each other at your native worths.

Dimsdell. I shall be glad to know you better, Doctor.

Roger. And I, to see you better, sir.

Dimsdell. Pardon me, I must in; I'm late already.

Exit Dimsdell—all follow except Governor Bellingham and Roger Prynne. Bell ceases.

Governor. How weak a hold we have on health! That man

Is but the standing ruin of his former self,

And yet, for beauty, comeliness and grace,

He still is model to the colony.

What do you think, can care restore him yet,

And give him to us as he used to be?

Roger. I cannot tell. I need more knowledge of him.

There are no marks of cureless malady—

A faint suggestion of overwatchfulness,

That oft points out the student—nothing more.

Hymn from church. (Tune: "Ein' feste Burg" or other ancient hymn used by the Puritans.)

Governor. The worship hath begun; but, ere we in,

A word about the wealth you left with me.

Roger. No more. Pray use it as your own, in trade,

Or howsoe'er you choose. The largest pearl

An Indian chief did give me; but sell it with

The rest, and with their worth provide for Hester.

She is the widow of mine ancient friend,

To whom I ever shall be much indebted,

And while I would not have her know me yet

As what I am—her husband's friend and hers—

As that might breed more grief in her, or wake

An old one—yet I think it meet to care

For her and for her child.

Governor. Your goodness is

Your passport, Doctor. Come, let us in.—Nay,

After you; you are my guest.

[*Exeunt.*

Scene III.

Bed room of the Rev. Arthur Dimsdell. *Night.* Dimsdell, *alone in the dark.*

Dimsdell. O, she is beautiful!

The memory of her loveliness

Pervades my waking dreams, and, pleasant theft,

Deprives my sleep of dark oblivion.

And thus, while fleeing from the gentle bonds

Of love, I am become the thrall of passion,

And sigh my heart away in waste desire!

Had I but truly loved her,

Would not our joys, that then were innocent,

Have moulded soul to soul and made mine take

The form of her most dear perfections?

But, now!

No trait of Hester's noble purity

Remains with guilty me, for I purloined

Her precious diadem and like a rogue

I cast that crown away, afraid to wear

What would have been my dearest ornament.

Why can I not repent? Or is it true

Repentance is denied the hypocrite?

And must it then forever be that, though

I cast out sin, both root and branch, the seed

Of evil, scattered long ago, will sprout

And bloom carnation thoughts that dull the soul

With subtle sweetness!

Oh! coward that I am!

Bound down, as to a rock, to form and place,

By iron chains of worldly precedent,

While my desires like eagles tear my breast,

And make of me a base Prometheus.

O, God!

I married all the family of sins,

When I espoused the pleasantest; I am

Become a liar through my lechery,

A thief of reputation through my cowardice,

And—puh! the rest but follow in the train

Of my dear wedded crime!

O, God! and shall this lust burn on in me

Still unconsumed? Can flagellation, fasting,

Nor fervent prayer itself, not cleanse my soul

From its fond doting on her comeliness?

Oh! heaven! is there no way for me to jump

My middle age and plunge this burning heart

Into the icy flood of cold decay?

None? O, wretched state of luxury!

This hot desire grows even in its death

And from its ashes doth arise full fledged

Renewed eternally!

A blinding flash of lightning, followed quickly by sharp thunder, discloses Dimsdell kneeling at his couch, and also shows SATAN*—an archangel with bat wings—who has just entered.*

Have mercy upon me, O, my God, have mercy!

According to thy gentle lovingkindness,

According to the multitude of all

Thy tender mercies, blot out my foul transgression.

Purge me with hyssop, and I shall be clean;

Wash me, and I shall be whiter than snow;

Hide thy face from my sins, and blot out

All mine iniquities.

Satan. You mar the psalm, Sir priest, for you omit

The saving clause. Your sin is unconfessed.

Dimsdell. Who art thou that durst interpose between

My soul and God?

Satan. I am the stronger part of lower nature,

The worser part of all that came from Him

Whom all adore. Behold me!

Satan becomes visible by light emanating from himself.

Dimsdell. Thou art Satan! The Prince of Hell!

Satan. I am so called.

Dimsdell. Get thee hence! I am a minister

Of God, a priest, and am anointed of the Lord

To teach His children.

Satan. And, therefore, am I come to thee, Sir priest.

I do confess a predilection for

Thy calling; conclaves, synods, convocations,

Are never held without my guiding presence;

They are my field days and my exercises,
While in the study and the cell I take
My cloistered ease. I love all priests and am
The bosom friend of many who would blush
To speak to me in public. Receive me, brother.

Dimsdell. Scorner, avaunt! Sink to the hell from whence
Thou cam'st! I do abhor thee, Satan; yea,
I tell thee to thy face that I who quail
Before the awful majesty of God,
And cowardly do hide my sin from man,
I tell thee, vile as I am, I do detest
Thy very name! I do defy thee!

Satan. These words are very brave; if more than wind,
Go to the market place tomorrow, there
Proclaim thy vice; or else ascend thy pulpit
And denounce thyself as what thou art, adulterer.

Dimsdell. Recreant to my God am I; think'st thou
That I will thee obey, to whom I owe
No deep allegiance?

Satan. Then bare thy sinful breast, for here I swear,
By that dread Name which mortals cannot hear,
I will upon thee print a mark, the stigma
Of thy secret crime.

Dimsdell. Hold off! I charge thee by that other Name

Of Him who rent thy kingdom, and will destroy it,

Touch me not yet!

Almighty Purity, Dread Essence Increate;

Behold concentrate, in this wicked form,

The universal spirit of iniquity.

Come quickly in thy majesty, O Lord!

Wither him here within the awful flame

Of Thy bright Holiness! Shrivel his frame

Into an atom, and blow the lifeless dust

Beyond the farthest star.

And, if in his destruction my soul should share

Through close proximity, spare not!

Then will Thy servants serve Thee, Gracious Lord!

And mankind find its paradise!

Satan. That was well said!

Perhaps, Sir priest, you now will treat me to

A learned disquisition on the birth

Of evil? I'd like to hear it, if it tread

Beyond theology's well beaten path;

But, if it stumbles in the pug-mill round

Of teleology, you must excuse me.

Dimsdell. Base siege of scorn! I curse thee!

Satan. Curses but belch foul wind, they pass beyond me.

But, come; I have no time to waste with thee;

This visitation had not been, nor would

I dignify thy carnal slip by my

Incarnate presence, but for thy perfidy.

For thou hast reached a depth of moral baseness

Below the meanest fiend in lowest hell;

Thou hast deserted her who sinned with thee,

Gave up her virtue to express her love,

Laid down her treasure to thy secret lust,

And then took up thy burden with her own.

Think not I come to draft thee of my legions,

I would not have so weak, so mean a coward,

To sow pale fear among them. No!

Thou wilt be damned outside of Hell. I come

To show, as in a mirror, what thou art;

Not what thou shalt be. The past and present both

Are mine, the future rests with God. But now,

Hester's image appears in a cloud dressed in white.

Behold the woman as thou first didst know her,

A loveliness to tempt or saint or devil,

The rare quintessence of pure womanhood!

Transparent brightness! A living crystal globe,

Wherein all beauties of humanity

Reflect themselves with iridescent glow!

Dost thou remember?

Behold her now the mother of thy babe,

The image of Hester changes. She holds their babe in her arms.

Whose pretty wiles would win hard Moloch's heart;

Make him forget his rites, and turn man-nurse.

O, fool! I would renounce my war with Heaven,

Eat up my pains in one most bitter mouthful,

And sue for pardon from God's hated Throne,

If such an offspring might but call me father!

Where is thy manly pride?

But, now, behold her shamed, bearing the badge

Hester's image wears Scarlet Letter "A."

Of thy foul infamy. Tear wide thy shirt,

For as thou look'st on her I will impress

Upon thy breast a stigma worse than hers.

Aye, fall upon thy knees to worship her

The Lady of the Scarlet Letter.

Yet while thou kneel'st thy flesh doth glow and burn

Scarlet Letter "A" glows on Dimsdell's breast.

With all the deep red heraldry befits

A coward lust: the latter "A" in gules

Upon thy sable heart. There let it gnaw

Forever and forever!

Hester vanishes. Satan fades. No light, save "A" on Dimsdell's breast.

And, now I go, I put this curse upon thee:

Be coward still, wear outwardly the garb

Of righteousness, shake in thy pious shoes,

Cover the stigma on thy breast from eyes

Of flesh, and be a hypocrite, till death

Relieves the world of thee. We'll meet again.

[*Lightning. Exit Satan. Dimsdell lies in trance.*

Night. No sound, no light.

Act III.

Scene I.

The garden of Governor Bellingham. ROGER PRYNNE, *called Chillingworth, alone.*

Roger. The fox that robbed my roost is sly; he keeps

The cover warily; and, now the scent

Is cold, the curs that yelp in scandal's pack

Bay loud on many faults, but cannot trace him.

Enter DIGGORY.

Diggory. Doctor, the Governor will join you presently.

Roger. Diggory, I will await him patiently.

[Sits.

Diggory retires, then returns.

Diggory. Doctor, may I beg a word with you?

Roger. A thousand if you will.

Diggory. I would speak in confidence.

Roger. The manner would become thee, Diggory. But speak, man! Say on.

Diggory. I need a philter, Doctor. For the love of mercy—

Roger. For the love of good liquor, Diggory, thou shalt have twenty filters. Still decanting?

Diggory. O, sir! not that kind of filter. I'm in love!

Roger. Ah! thou art in love? In love didst thou say?

Diggory. Aye, sir, if it please you.

Roger. It pleases me well enough; how doth it please the lady?

Diggory. She's not a lady, sir, thank God! she's but a simple maiden, and it pleaseth her not.

Roger. A simple maid refuses you! Ah! Diggory, Diggory, be thankful for the good things God hath sent thee.

Diggory. Truly, sir, I thank Him ev'ry day; but, sir, as I do desire the maiden—I—I—would have her too.

Roger. And so, Diggory, thou wouldst have me aid thee in this folly, and give thee a love potion?

Diggory. Aye, sir, begging your honor's pardon.

Roger. But why dost thou ask me, Diggory? Dost thou take me for an herb-doctor, or a necromancer, or what?

Diggory. My master, the Governor, says you are a very learned man, a what-you-call-'em—a scientist; and a scientist can do anything.

Roger. Humph!—Diggory, I do not deal in philters; they are out of date—but I know a charm will win her love.

Diggory. Tell it me for the love of—

Roger. Thou wilt betray it, Diggory.

Diggory. Never! Never!

Roger. Omit thou but a word of it, and the maiden's lost to thee—but con it well, and all her beauties will be thine.

Diggory. Oh! Doctor!

Roger. Take of the rendered grease of three black bears—do not fail in that—anoint thy curly locks—

Diggory. My hair is straight.

Roger. Never mind—but rub; and, as thou dost, repeat these words:

Lady love, lady love, where e'er thou be,

Think of no man but only me;

Love me, and wed me, and call me thine own,

Ting-a-ling, ting-a-ling, ting-a-ling, Joan.

Diggory. What is that "Ting-a-ling, ting-a-ling"?

Roger. That is the chief element of the charm—don't forget it. Having done this on nine successive days—dost thou follow me?

Diggory. Aye, sir.

Roger. On the tenth go to the barber's and have thy hair cut short.

Diggory. But, sir, my hair is my best feature!

Roger. It is with many; cut it, however, or lose the worth of all of the charm. Dost thou hear, Diggory? Cut thy hair short or never win fair woman. Farewell.

Diggory. I thank you, sir. [*Going]* "Lady love, ting-a-ling"—nay, that's not it.

Roger. Diggory!

Diggory. Yes, sir.

Roger. Who are with the Governor?

Diggory. The worthy ministers, Master Wilson and Master Dimsdell.

Roger. Very well.

[*Exit Diggory, trying to recall the verse.*

Ah! Diggory, thou art but a dram of love in a fluid ounce of fool! And so may we label all mankind. For instance: the Governor is a wise man and a politic; Wilson a good man and a pious; Dimsdell—ah! there I pause, for what fine formula can sum the qualities of that same Arthur Dimsdell? He's not a fool; nor mad; nor truly cataleptic—yet he's moody, falls in trance, and I suspect his power as a preacher comes from ecstasy. Something he is akin to genius—yet he hath it not, for though his aim be true enough, he often flashes in the pan when genius would have hit the mark. I'll write his case in Latin! What a study that would be if I could first find out the reason why he clutches at his breast!—If once I find him in a trance, alone—ah! here they come.

Enter Governor Bellingham, Rev. John Wilson, Rev. Arthur Dimsdell, *and following them, with a tray of wine*, Diggory.

Wilson. Good morrow, Doctor.

Roger. Good morning, gentlemen.

Governor. [*To Diggory.*] Leave the wine within the summer house. Good morning, Doctor. When Mistress Prynne doth come conduct her hither.

Diggory. Sir, she's coming this way now.

Governor. Very well. Go. [*Exit Diggory.*] Doctor, we debate what disposition should be made of Hester Prynne's young child. We ask your aid—but here she is.

Enter HESTER PRYNNE.

Hester. Your worship hath been pleased to summon me

To bring my child before you.

Governor. Where is the child?

Hester. The babe is sick but answers by attorney.

What is your will?

Governor. Some pious matrons, Hester,

Have charged that thou art not a person fit

To rear that infant immortality,

And guide it unto God.

Hester. God gave the child

In rich exchange for all things else which I,

Poor sinful I, had forfeited; and now

You, who have made yourselves the flails of God,

Would separate the wheat from chaff before

The grain is ripe, and take her from me.

Oh! ye are wise! No doubt ye see beyond
The purpose of Almighty God who gave
The child to me!

Governor. Nay, take it not to heart,
For, Hester, duty to the child we owe
To put its soul upon the way that leads
To Heaven. She will be cared for tenderly.

Hester. She is the last small link that binds my soul
To earth, the tiny needle that doth point
My way to Heaven. You shall not take her from me!
Speak thou for me [*To Dimsdell*]; as my pastor speak;
Speak now; and say if any harm from me
Will hurt the child. I will not part with her!
Say if thou canst, for thou hast sympathies
Which these men lack, say what the mother's rights
Are in her child; and what those rights must be
When naught beside the child is left to her—
Her husband gone, her friends deserted,
No reputation, no sympathy, no love—
But only those twin brands of shame, her baby
And The Scarlet Letter!

Dimsdell. I have a dual duty to discharge;
I am this woman's pastor—and her friend,

And therefore she hath called me to defend her;

I am, beside, a member of your council,

And hence am with you in your consultation;

And yet, I think, these duties may be made

To yoke and draw me to a just conclusion.

Wilson. Thou also hast a duty to the child.

Dimsdell. Aye, so I have. Our aim is well enough,

But let us pause before we do adopt

A means that varies from the one marked out

By God and Nature.

Governor. Is there not command

To teach our children in the fear of God

And guide them from impurity?

Dimsdell. God gave us mothers when He gave us life,

And to their tender care He did entrust

The mortal and immortal parts of us.

What then? Would we improve upon His system;

Would we now deprive this little one

Of that fond mother-care which nurtures her?

Or would we put, in place of mother-love,

The cold, hard, formal training of a paid

Instructor?

Governor. But is this woman, stained with sin,

A mother to entrust a child to?

Dimsdell. That question God hath answered; and we know

The stain of sin doth fade beneath the bleach

Of true repentance; through it all appears

The woven figure of the woman-fabric—

Her motherhood!

We owe our lives to woman's suffering,

We owe our health unto her temperance,

We owe her all the best of us. Let God

Condemn her sin, but let us not presume

To punish her where He hath healed her heart.

Wilson. There is weight in what he says.

Roger. Yea, and earnestness!

Governor. Well, Hester, go thy way; the child is thine.

Remember thou dost owe a gentle thanks

Unto this pious man. Go, Hester, keep

The child. Think well upon his words; be thou

A mother in all righteousness, as well

As in thy sin. Farewell.

Hester. I thank you, gentlemen.

[*Exit*.

Wilson. That woman would have been a noble wife

Had not some villain robbed her of her dower.

Governor. Come, gentlemen, this business well is ended,

And, Dimsdell, yours is all the credit of it;

For one I thank you.

Roger. We all do thank you, sir.

Governor. Come, let us drain a cup of wine; and then

Go in.

Dimsdell. I beg you to excuse me.

Roger. And me,

I pray. I'll stay with Dimsdell.

Governor. Well, Wilson, you

Shall not escape me. Gentlemen, the wine

We leave you; keep it company.—And, Dimsdell,

Forget it not, to-morrow thou must preach

A grand election sermon. The people do

Expect a master effort, man. Fail not.

[*Exeunt Governor and Wilson.*

Roger. He will not fail them, Governor; a tongue

Of flame is his. What ails thee, Dimsdell?

How now? Why man!

Dimsdell. I'm very weak. The pain about my heart—

Roger. Nay, courage, man! 'Twill leave thee soon. I'll get a cup of wine to cheer thee up.

Dimsdell. Do, I pray. And, Doctor, give me something to abate this agony.

Roger. I will.

[*Exit.*

Dimsdell. Try how I may, there's no escape from pain.

I robbed the law's strong arm, and thereby put

The lash in conscience' hand—and yet I thought

Hypocrisy a duty to my calling!

'Twere better I were known as what I am,

Than still to hide my sin beneath the garb

Of outward purity! 'Twere better now,

By Hester's side, to bear opprobrium,

And brave what man may do, than still to nurse

This misery in secret!

Re-enter Roger *with wine-tray; places it upon a bench and, taking a vial from a pocket medicine-case, pours a few drops into a wine-glass, then fills the glass with wine.*

Roger. A minim more would lull him into sleep.

Here is the chance—and here the will—to learn

His secret malady. What holds me back?

Conscience? Tut, tut! It will not harm him!

'Twill do him good to sleep; 'twill do me good

To know the why he clutches at his breast.

I'll do it.

[*Pours more from vial.*

Sir, drink this off.

Dimsdell. I thank thee, kind physician.

[*Drinks.*

Roger. Nay, thank me not. Now, take a glass of wine.

[*Giving him another glass.*

Dimsdell. Methinks, the wine is richer than is common.

Roger. Thirst always gives an added age to wine.

This is right Xeres. Hast been in Spain?

Dimsdell. Nay, but the wine hath. I feel its warmth.

Roger. Truly, it is a grand inquisitor;

'Twill search each petty heresy that taints

Thy blood, and burn it to a cinder.

Dimsdell. How many leagues it came to serve my need.

Roger. Aye, a thousand, and a thousand more!

Dimsdell. I would not go so far for it just now,

For through my limbs there creeps a lang'rous ease

Like that which doth precede deep slumber.

Roger. Rest here upon this bench.

[*Dimsdell sits, half reclining.*

Give way unto your drowsiness; it is

Not sleep, but rest and relaxation. There!

I'll keep you company.

Dimsdell. Do.

Roger. [*Pouring wine and drinking*.] This wine is liquid gold.

I quaff to your good health and ease of mind.

This is good wine. It warms my chilly blood

With all the dreamy heat of Spain. I hear

The clack of th' castinet and th' droning twang

Of stringéd instruments; while there before

Mine eyes brown, yielding beauties dance in time

To the pulsing music of a saraband!

And yet there is a flavor of the sea,

[*Sipping wine.*

The long-drawn heaving of the ocean wave,

The gentle cradling of a tropic tide;

Its native golden sun—I fear you sleep?

Or do the travels of the wine so rock

Your soul that self is lost in revery?

Why, man, dream not too much of placid bliss;

Nor wine, nor man, can reach this clear perfection

Until they pass the rack of thunder and

Of hurricane.—'Tis on us now! Awake!

[*Shouting in Dimsdell's ear.*

My friend, awake! Dost thou not hear the storm?

Oh! how it shrieks and whistles through the shrouds!

The awful guns of heaven boom in our ears—

Nay, that was the mainsail gone by the board,

Flapping with cannon roar.

You do not follow me. O, come, I say!

This is no sermon. You cannot be asleep,

Yet feign you are to cheat me of my story.

Wake up, my friend. You carry the jest too far.

Roger cautiously shakes Dimsdell.

So soon! So sound!

[*Looks around.*

I fear you are not easy; thus. That's better.

Your pardon, sir, your collar's much too tight.

Now will I steal his hidden mystery,

And learn the secret of his lengthened pain;

Cure him and gain great honor. To think a man

Would case himself in buttons like an armour!

Now, shirt——

Merciful God! what miracle is this!

A stigma! Aye! a stigma! the letter "A"

In blood suffused! The counterpart of that

Which Hester wears, but palpitating here

In life! This is beyond my skill.

Ah! David! David! Thou art the man! Thou wouldst

Have set me in the hot forefront of battle

Hadst thou but known me as Uriah!

Bah!

Why, what a brainless dullard have I been,

To see this pretty puff-ball of a preacher

Wax large before mine eyes in righteous husk—

And think him whole within—when but a touch,

But one, had aired his rottenness!

Oh! dotard that I am! blind, deaf and stupid!

It takes a miracle to make me see

What lay before me open. He did take

Her part; ever professed himself her friend;

And at her trial fell in trance. What more?

He is the man! He is the man!

Now ends our game of hoodman blind; oh, I

Was warm, so very warm at times, so hot,

Did almost touch thee; yet I knew thee not

For him I sought. Thou cunning hypocrite!

It must be I am fitted to my state,

Dull, trusting and incapable;

Or else—why surely I'm a fool.—

Had I been here when Hester bore her child,

I would have fondly dreamed it was mine own;

Put on the unearned pride that old men wear

When their young wives bear children.

A pretty baby, sir! My grandchild?—No;

Mine own; my very own! Nay, wrong me not;

I'm not so old—not so damned old after all!

A ghe! a ghoo! Are not the eyes like mine?—

Yea, would have dandled it upon my knee,

And coddled each succeeding drop, as though

My fires had distilled them.

But—now I know—my knowledge must be hid.

Back shirt! cover blazoned infamy

And let the whited front still hide from man

The sepulchre of crime that festers here.

He will not wake within an hour. I'll go

Inform the Governor he sleeps, and have

Him order none disturb his pious rest.

Then I'll return and calmly probe his soul.

Sleep on! Sleep on!

[*Exit Roger.*

Scene II.

Another part of the garden. Enter alone, Diggory.

Diggory. If there be no true charm but it hath a touch of folly in it, this one must be most potent. Now a wise man would not think there's that virtue in a bit of grease, a jingling rhyme, and a hair cut, that one might thereby win a woman's love—but the wise are fools in love. I have here the lard of three bears—one more than the old adage of "bear and forbear"—and with it I am to anoint my head as an enchantment to bring about my marriage to Betsey—marry, I'll temper the strength of the charm with a little bergamot, for in truth two of the bears have been dead over-long. Whew!—Aha! enchantment is the only highway to success in love! Now let me see: "Lady love, lady love, where'er you be"—

Betsey. [Singing behind the scenes]

Little bird, little bird, come tell me true;

If I love my love, as your love loves you,

And if he loves me, as you love your mate;

Can hardly be called, sirs, quite sober.

Diggory. That's Betsey singing now! If the charm works like this, bear fat will be worth its weight in gold. But perhaps my features may have pleased her after all—I'm not bad to look upon; and truly I would save my hair; it's the best part about me. Singing again.

Betsey. [*Singing behind the scenes*]

In Summer-tide, sweet Summer-tide,

O, what can a maiden do,

If, while he walks close by her side,

Her lover begins to woo?

Diggory. Now I wonder where she learnt all those profane songs? From some liberal folk in the old country, no doubt; they ill become a puritan. If she were a little slower in her speech, what an angel she would be! As it is, she is a very good woman, tongue and all.

Betsey. [*Singing again, behind the scenes.*]

For her, of buttercups and violets,

A circlet for her hair he makes;

And sings, in roundelays and triolets,

A song that soon her fancy takes.

In Summer-tide, sweet Summer-tide,

O, what can a maiden do,

If, while he walks close by her side,

Her lover begins to woo?

Diggory. I'm not a judge of songs, but if she means half she says—and a woman sometimes does—some one is about to be the top feather in Fortune's cap; it may be me. I'll try my luck once more. [*Going toward R. wing*] Why, here she comes.

Enter Betsey, *with a pair of butter paddles.*

Betsey. [*Entering.*]

Adown the moonlit path they walk,

Through all the world called lover's lane,

And hand in hand they sigh and talk

Of the love that binds them, happy twain!

What are you gaping like a great gaby for?

Diggory. For Fortune to drop the plum into my mouth.

Betsey. Where is the plum?

Diggory. There. [*Pointing at her.*]

Betsey. You silly fellow! yesterday I was a peach; the day before strawberries and cream; the day before that a rose; and last week a dove—marry, I don't coo for you! Can I be all these things at once and still be Betsey Tomkins?

Diggory. O, Betsey, thou art all the world to me!

Betsey. O, Diggory, thou art a great fool to me! Why, man, thy head is as soft as a pat of butter; I could take it between my paddles, like this, and mold it into any shape I chose.

Diggory. So you may, Betsey; so you may. And, Betsey, for the love of mercy, mold it into the head of thy future husband.

Betsey. 'Twould take a pair of shears to do that.

Diggory. Wouldst thou marry me, Betsey, if I should lose my pretty locks?

Betsey. I would not marry you with them, that's flat.

Diggory. Shall I shave my head or only clip it close?

Betsey. Cut it off, Diggory, cut it off.

Diggory. Kiss me but once, Betsey, and I'll cut my head off; 'tis of little use to me now, and if thou dost marry me—well, thy head shall rest upon my shoulder, like this, and one head is enough for any pair of shoulders.

Betsey. *In Summer-tide, sweet Summer-tide,*

O, what can a maiden do, etc.

[*Exeunt.*

Scene III.

The same as in Scene I of this act. Dimsdell asleep upon a garden bench, half reclining. Enter Roger Prynne, *called Chillingworth.*

Roger. To kill were easy; aye, but—to stretch his life

As on a rack—were that not better still?

Dead, I'd bury with him my revenge;

But while he lives the old account will stand

At daily usury.

I'll tent his agony, prolong it here,

Even here where I may feed upon it;

Not send him hence beyond my reach. Aye!

I'll fight with death to keep him for mine own.

But, now—

O, I must calm myself or miss my aim!

For, like a hunter when first he sees the buck,

My nerves are all unstrung. This weakling trick

Of overearnestness betrays the fool

In me; and yet we know it, though we profit not,

The eager hand doth ever spill the cup

That lifted carefully would quench our thirst.

I must assume a wise placidity;

As he puts on—Ah! damnéd hypocrite!—

The air of purity. (*Approaches Dimsdell.*)

I'll drink dissimulation at the source;

I'll study him.—Thus might an angel look

When, wearied with the music of the spheres,

He laid him down upon a roseate bank

To dream of holiness!—He hath not stirred.—

'Twas well I did not speak to Bellingham,

For we have not been noted. Good, so far.

All eyes are busy with their own affairs;

I'll wake him now and foil discovery.

Takes vial from pocket medicine case.

Our native drugs are balanced well; one plant

Sucks in the beams the sleepy moon sends down,

Another drinks the waking draught of dawn.

That made him sleep, but this—Ah!

A mouldy mummied corse that in the tomb

A thousand years had lain, would wake once more,

If but three drops of this should touch its lips.

I'll give you, sir, but two.

Drops liquid into glass and fills with wine.

There, swallow it.

Administering to Dimsdell.

Now, let me see—he must not know how long

He slept,—and by the sun it is not long—

I have't; I'll make him think he merely lost

Himself while I was talking.

Dimsdell stirs. Roger pours a glass of wine and takes position he occupied when Dimsdell fell asleep. Speaks as in continuation of former speech.

Mellow wine

Is Nature's golden bounty unto man.

And it hath well been said: Dame Nature is

A gentle mother if we follow her;

But if she drives our steps no fury wields

A fiercer lash; yet all her punishments

Are kindly meant; our puny faculties

Would nest forever fledgeling in our minds,

Did not her wise austerity compel

Their flight.

Dimsdell wakes with a start and recovers himself as one who would not seem rude.

Or, put the same in other words:

That man is noble who doth fear no fate

Which may afflict humanity; but, like

A gallant soldier, meets the charge half way,

And takes his wounds a-jesting.

Now ev'ry one of us, whom Nature whips,

Must take it meekly; for she means our good;

And learn to go along with her.

Dimsdell. I fear

I dozed and lost the thread of argument.

I pray you, pardon me.

Roger. I did not note it.

But, be it so, come sun yourself; drive out

The fog and vapor that becloud your mind,

And let the warmth of nature take their place.

Nature retrieves our losses, or charges them

Against us; all things do rest, even the plants

Do slumber as they grow.

Dimsdell. How greedily

The flow'rs drink up the wine our golden sun

Pours down on them, yet blush to own their drinking!

Roger. This is the New World, man; and Nature here

Is lusty; drink in thy dole of heat and light;

For even I, drenched in the golden rain,

Feel pulsings of lost paradise that make

My blood leap with th' quick-step bound of youth.

This is the very show'r of gold in which

Jove comes to fill the longing world with life.

And as he kisses her with ling'ring lips,

All Nature lies wide open to th' warm embrace

And quickens in his arms.—All, all, but thou!

For thou art single as the northern pole;

As cold, as distant, and unreachable

To what hath passion's warmth; and, though

Thy life be at its summer solstice—bright

With day—thy heart still turns to barren ice,

More bleak than many a wintry age.

Dimsdell. How can I change my disposition, Doctor?

Roger. Widen the thin ecliptic of thy life;

Revolve upon another axis, man;

Let love, the sun of life, beam meltingly

Upon thy heart and thaw it into happiness.

Marry, man, marry.

Dimsdell. I cannot marry: I have my work to do.

Roger. If work precedent were to love, the world

Would be unpeopled. This is the month of June,

And now the locust and the linden tree

Do wed the zephyrs as they blow, and weight

The air with oversweetness.—What song is that?

[*Voice of Betsey singing behind scenes.*]

For her, of buttercups and violets,

A circlet for her hair he makes;

And sings, in roundelays and triolets,

A song that soon her fancy takes.

In Summer-tide, sweet Summer-tide,

O, what can a maiden do,

If, while he walks close by her side,

Her lover begins to woo?

Roger. That maid is innocent and happy too.

You may have noticed that—when the heart

Is pure—love overflows the lips in song

As sweet and limpid as a mountain spring;

But—when it's bitter with base treachery—

It dams itself against all utterance,

And either mines the soul, or, breaking forth,

Sweeps downward to destruction. Oh! 'tis true,

Love is the lyric happiness of youth;

And they, who sing its perfect melody,

Do from the honest parish register

Still take their tune. And so must you. For you

Are now in the very period of youth

When myriads of unborn beings knock loud and long

Upon the willing portals of the heart

For entrance into life. Deny it not;

I say but truth—I once was young myself.

Behold the means!

Enter MARTHA WILSON, *carrying a bunch of roses.*

Dimsdell. Oh! Oh! [*Clasps his breast.*]

Roger. Whither so fast, Martha, that thou canst not speak to us?

Martha. Oh! I beg your pardon, Doctor. Good morning, sir. I seek my father; is he with the Governor?

Roger. Knowledge is costly, Martha; yet thou art rich enough to buy more than information. For one of those sweet roses, I'll tell you he is well and with the Governor.

Martha. You beg it prettily.

[*Giving Roger a rose.*

Roger. Pure and fragrant as the giver—marry, the blush becomes it not so well; it does not come and go. Martha, thy father and the Governor are in the library. Is that not worth another rose?

Martha. Nay, only a very little one; for when he talks of books he's always loath to come with me.

Roger. Nay, slander him not. But, Martha, books or no books, for two more roses I will bring him here; and, truly, fathers were cheap at three roses apiece. What say you?

Martha. Nay, I'll go myself; but do not think I grudge the roses; here they are. You have not begged of me [*To Dimsdell*]. May I beg you to accept this? Gentlemen, farewell.

[Exit Martha.

Roger. Roses, and you asked her not!

In love! in love! up to the eyes in love!

She'll drown in love unless you marry her!

Dimsdell. Oh! that I were worthy of her!

Roger. Dost love her, Dimsdell? Ah! she's worthy love.

She's fair and young; of gentle birth and rich;

And warm and pure and spirit-like as flame

That floats above new brandy.

Dimsdell. Out upon thee, satyr! Thou dishonorest her.

Roger. Not a whit. Is't dishonor to her purity

To urge thy smoky flame to brightness worthy

Of her? 'Tis what she wishes most; witness

Her confusion and her telltale blushes.

Do me justice, man; my thoughts are pure

And dwell on lawful marriage only. Thou, thou

Alone, couldst see impurity in that.

I spoke of thee, man, of thee; and who

Beside thyself would think a mottled thought

Could touch a maiden linked to thee in words

Or fact?

Dimsdell. Oh! Oh!

[*Clutching at his breast.*

Roger. Had I young daughters by the score, each fair

As Hebe, as voluptuous as Venus,

All thinly clad as in the golden age,

I could not wish a chaster keeper of them.

Nay, had I wives in droves like Solomon,

I'd make thee Kislah Aga of my harem,

Chief eunuch and sole security—What!

Call me satyr when I urge in bounds

The boundless beauties of pure maidenhood,

And bid thee wed them! Thus best advices are

Construed amiss, and what we kindly mean

Turned into scorn and filthiness!

Dimsdell. Forgive me, Doctor; I'm ill at ease. This pain

Is like a stick thrust in a spring; it muddies

All my thoughts. Oh! Oh!

[*Pressing his hands to his breast.*

Roger. Come, Dimsdell, listen to a bit of reason.

Thy body is as sound as a red apple

In November. The pain's imaginary.

Marry, man, marry; thy wife will prove

A counter-irritant and drive the pain away.

Dimsdell. No more of that, I pray you.

Roger. Not enough of it, not enough of it!

Dimsdell. No more, no more! I must not marry.

Roger. Think once again, man; if that thy mind
Can pardon the suggestion—and, mark, I urge it
With all diffidence—there is a way,
Wherein the low opinion thou doth hold
Of thine own virtues—not held by any else—
May wed with beauty all unspeakable,
Raise up a noble lady, and show thy christian
Spirit to the world.

Dimsdell. And what is that?

Roger. Wed Hester Prynne.

Dimsdell. Wed Hester Prynne?

Roger. Aye! 'twas that I said.
She is a paragon—nay, beauty's self.
All other women are but kitchen-maids
Beside her loveliness.

Dimsdell. Wed Hester Prynne!

Roger. I hear her husband left her well to do;

And as for that small blot that sullies her

'Twill fade when covered by thy name.

Dimsdell. Hester Prynne!

Roger. What act more merciful, more christianlike?

Redeem the reputation of her child,

And to the jeers of fools stop up thine ears;

Enwrap thee in her gentle arms, lay down

Thine aching head upon her tender breast,

And dream thyself in paradise.

Dimsdell. Thou fiend of Hell! I know thee now; thou cam'st

But once in thine own form, and ever since

Hast been too near me in a worser one.

Back to the pit, I say! No more of tempting!

Roger. Art mad? I'm man as thou dost seem to be;

I'm not a fiend.

Dimsdell. What dost thou know?

[*Shaking Roger by the shoulders.*

Roger. Only this—thou art as cowardly

As thou art lecherous. What! betray

A woman! Desert her in her misery!

Refuse to marry her!

And all the while, cloaked in thy ministry,

Dispense the sacraments of God to children—

How canst thou do it?

Dimsdell. If thou be not Satan, why raise this cloud?

Why vanish from my sight? Yet I did touch him even now—

I'll kill him—Kill, kill, kill—now, now, now—

Roger. In trance again! Help! Help! Help!

Dimsdell becomes rigid; with arm uplifted as if to strike a death blow. His speech thickens, and he stands motionless. Roger supports him.

Act IV.

Scene I.

A room. DIMSDELL *upon a couch in a cataleptic trance.* ROGER PRYNNE *watching him. Two chairs; other furniture heavy and immovable.*

Roger. [*Feeling Dimsdell's pulse*] There's been no change.

A very long trance.

At times he mumbles; at other times, as now,

He lies like death. If ev'ry murderer

Were stricken with the image of the thing

Which he would deal, 'twould be a blessing! Yet

When consciousness returns, with it will come

The murderous disposition; for in these cases

The mind, although it wanders while the trance

Is on, always comes back upon its path

Where first it left It. Therefore, 'twere wise in me

To be on guard. Well, so I am; but what—

What fear should drive me hence, or make me leave

The study of his case? He hath no arms

But such as both of us were born with;

And despite my age I am his equal that way.

Ah! a chair swung by a furious man

Might make an omelet of my brain;

Therefore, one chair will do—and that for me.

[Removes chair.

Enter GOVERNOR BELLINGHAM *in robes of office.*

Governor. Good morning, Doctor.

Roger. Good morning, Governor. I wish you, sir,

As happy and as prosperous a term

In office, as that just closing.

Governor. I thank you, sir.

Has Dimsdell recovered from his trance?

Roger. Not yet. There he lies.

Governor. Wonderful!

Can you account for his condition, Doctor?

Roger. There's no accounting for it, Governor.

This is the second trance I've seen him in;

How many more he's had, God only knows.

Governor. 'Tis most unfortunate that we must lack

His eloquence to-day. The people, who

Always love high-sounding words more than

Wise thoughts, prefer the music of his voice

To good old Wilson's drone. Why isn't he in bed?

Roger. Oh! there are many reasons; 'twould take too long

To tell you now; but at another time

I'll ask your patience for a tale more strange

Than ever made your flesh to creep.

Governor. Is there mystery in the case?

Roger. Mystery! aye, and miracle, too!

You know him, Governor—a man whose nerves

Are gossamers, too fine to sift the music

Of the blasts that blow about our burly world,

And only fit for harps whereon Zephyrus

In Elysium might breathe.—And yet this man—

Oh! you'd not believe it if I told you.

Enter Servant.

Servant. Your worship is asked for at the door.

Governor. Say I am coming. We'll speak again of this.

[Exit Servant.

I must be gone. We servants of the State

Are slaves to show, and serve the people best

When most we trick them. The pageant of the day

Goes much against my better judgment, but

The crowd will have it so, and so farewell.

Roger. One moment, if you please. If he revives

He'll pick the thread of life up where he dropt it;

He may desire to preach, as he hath promised you,

And, if he doth, 'twere better not to thwart him.

Governor. Very well. I'll speak to Wilson.

Roger. I'm sorry I cannot go with you. Farewell.

Exit Governor. Dimsdell moves. Roger goes to his side and examines him.

The pulse hath quickened. He moves his lips.

Dimsdell mumbles indistinctly.

I cannot catch it.—

Dimsdell. Think of it no more, my love.—

Our troubles now are ended, Hester;

The gentle current of our mingled lives,

Long parted by the barren, rocky isle

Of hard necessity, flows reunited on.

Roger. Indeed!

Dimsdell. How sweet it is, in the afternoon of life,

To walk thus, hand in hand, Hester. And as

The golden sun of love falls gently down

Into the purple glory of the West,

We'll follow it.

Roger. A lengthy jump—from sinning youth
Plump into the middle of an honored age!
Yet thus the mind, in trance or dream, achieves
Without an effort what it wills. Again?

Dimsdell. Sir, take my daughter and my blessing, too;
Cherish her as the apple of thine eye;
Still shield her from the buffets of the world;
Let thy tenderness breathe gentle love
Like an Italian air sung at twilight,
When the melody without tunes that within
Until the soul arising on the wings
Of music soars into Heaven.

Roger. Is there nothing in heredity? Or will
The orange-blossom take its fragrance from
The Heaven above; its origin forgot?

Dimsdell. Hester, although the snow upon thy head
Be white as that on yonder distant mount,
Thine eyes are blue and deep as Leman's lake
That lies before us.

Roger. Thus in our dreams we picture what we wish;
Not held to time or place; and while the body,
Like an anchor, sinks in mud, the wingéd craft

Swings with the tide of thought.

He's in Geneva now; Hester with him;

His daughter honorably married;

And all the pains of yesterday forgot.

I'll write it down.

[*Roger makes notes.*

Dimsdell. Good night, dear wife, good night.

The stars of Heaven melt into angel forms

Which stoop to lift me to the gates of bliss.

Farewell, farewell! Nay, weep not, Hester;

Our sins are now forgiven.

Yea, though I walk through the valley of th' shadow of death,

I will fear no evil.—Say it with me, Hester.

Roger. Will he die thus?

[*Examines Dimsdell.*

The pulse is weak—a clammy sweat—

'Tis but the culmination of the trance.

'Tis but a dream. A dream! Yet one must die;

And to our human thought that death were best

That came preceded by a flag of truce

To parley peace. To pass away in dreams—

Without the vain regret for work undone;

Without a load of sin to weight the soul;

With all the argentry of honored age

To frost our past; with all the fiercer heats

Of life burnt out into the cold, gray ash—

That were peace! Then might a man yield up

The willing ghost as calmly as a child

That falls asleep upon its mother's breast

To wake in paradise.

Dimsdell starts up.

Dimsdell. I see thee now—and now I'll kill, kill, kill—

If thou be Satan I cannot harm thee—

But if a man—

Dimsdell attempts to reach Roger, who keeps the one chair of the room in front of him and thus wards off Dimsdell.

Roger. Madman, listen! Thou canst not harm me, yet I am not Satan. My name is Roger Prynne. I am the husband of the woman you have wronged.

Dimsdell. Thou Roger Prynne?

Roger. Aye, Roger Prynne and thine accuser.

Dimsdell looks about the room as though dazed.

Dimsdell. Why, how is this?—But now, the Governor's garden—and now, my room!—But now, just now, old Doctor Chillingworth—and now, mine enemy, Roger Prynne! Thou art the Devil himself!—Thou shalt not trick me thus.

Band music in distance.

Roger. Trick thee? Why, madman, thou hast been in trance since yester noon. Trick thee! I like the word! 'Tis now the time of day when thou shouldst preach the great Election Sermon, the one event that makes or mars you preachers. Dost hear the music? A day hath passed since thou wast in the garden. They are marching even now to the market place.

Dimsdell. What shall I do?

[*Aloud, but to himself.*

Roger. Do? Stay here and settle our account; or else go on and publish thyself as what thou art—a hypocrite.

Dimsdell. I see it now!—Ah! Satan! Satan!—thou wouldst affright my soul and make me lose my well earned honors. Why, Roger Prynne is dead—dead. 'Twas told on good report two years ago. And now—oh! try it if thou wilt—I'll have thee burnt, burnt—burnt at the stake, if thou accusest me! Who would believe thee? Stand aside, I say! Let me pass!

Roger. How came the stigma on thy breast?

Dimsdell. Thou knowest!—Make way, I tell thee!—Thou didst place it there!—Make way!

They struggle. Roger interposes the chair between himself and Dimsdell. Finally, Dimsdell wrenches the chair from Roger, flings it aside, and, grappling him, chokes Roger to death.

Dimsdell. [Panting] A man! A man! A man!—Dead! dead! dead!—Nay—like a man!—Like a dead man!—A trick!—A devilish trick!—Did he not come in angel form—and then as Doctor Chillingworth—and then as Roger Prynne—and now,—and now, as a dead body?

Spurning Roger with his foot.

O, Devil, I'll avoid thee yet!—I'll confess my crime and thus unslip the noose about my soul!

Hurriedly prepares to depart.

He said we'd meet again! We have, and 'tis the last time!

[*Exit.*

Scene II.

Plain curtain, down. Music. Music ceases; subdued sounds as of a multitude back of curtain. Then the voice of Dimsdell rises as quiet returns.

Dimsdell. And now, good friends, Electors and Elected,

Although my speech hath run a lengthened course,

And what I purposed hath been said in full,

There's more comes to me now.

What is our purpose and our destiny?

Curtain rises rapidly, disclosing stage set as in Act I, Scene III. Dimsdell upon a rostrum on church steps. Militia standing at rest. Citizens and officials in gala attire.

We call us English, Anglo-Saxon;

And from the Old we come to build the New,

The equal England of our expectation.

Here in the wilderness, the first small germs

Of man's long-promised freedom find their soil;

Here hidden will they rot a little while;

Anon, the sprouts will break our troubled land,

Thrust forth the first red blades, and thence grow on,

Forever and forever!

I see this vast expanse of continent,

That dwarfs the noble states of cultured Europe,

Spread out before me like a map, from pole

To pole, and from the rising to the setting sun.

I see it teem with myriads; I see

Its densely peopled towns and villages;

I see its ports, greater than any known,

Send forth their riches to the hungry world.

I see, O blessed, wondrous sight! the strength

Of Anglo-Saxondom—our mighty England

And our great America, as one—

The Lion and the Eagle side by side,—

Leading the vanguard of humanity!

And more I see; I see the rise of man

Merely as man!

Let the day come, O Lord, when man, without

Addition to that noble title—man—

Can stand erect before his fellow-man,

Outface Oppression with his flashing eye,

And stamp and grind proud Tyranny to dust.

Put in our hearts, O, Gracious God, the yeast

Of freedom; let it work our natures free,

Although it break to recombine again

The atoms of each state.

Send down thy pulsing tongues of burning truth;

Fire our souls with love of human kind;

Let hate consume itself; let war thresh out

The brutal part of man, and fit us for

The last long period of peace.

A pause, then cries severally.

First Citizen. Is he an angel or a man? Sure Gabriel himself.

Second Citizen. Look! He faints.

Third Citizen. Poor minister!

Dimsdell. [*Rallying himself*] I will speak on.

Governor. My pious friend, wear not thy body out

To please our willing ears. Thou hast exceeded

Thy feeble strength already. Cease, man;

Demosthenes himself could not have stood

The strain which thou hast undergone. Prithee,—

Dimsdell. I thank you; reason not my wastefulness,

For, if you make me answer you, you cause

More waste. My taper's burnt already.

It flickers even now, and, ere I leave

This place, my light, my life will go.

Question me not,

For, now I have fulfilled my public function,

There hurries on a duty of a private kind

I must perform at once or not at all;

Too long delayed already.

My friends, my life is flowing fast away,

I, that should be at full or on the turn,

Am near my lowest ebb.

This gnawing at my heart hath eaten through,

And now my soul releasing body bondage

Will take its flight—but where?

First Citizen. It goes to Heaven when it flies;

But go not now.

Dimsdell. Behold yon woman with The Scarlet Letter.

Citizens. Oh, shame upon her! Fie!

Dimsdell. Nay, shame on me; her sufferings have made

Her pure, but mine, beneath this lying robe,

Have eaten up my heart. Hypocrisy

Lie there [*Taking off gown*]. Now, while I do descend these steps

I leave my former life behind.

Descends and goes toward pillory.

Come, Hester, come!

Come take my hand, although it be unworthy.

Second Citizen. Is the man mad, my masters?

Dimsdell. Not mad, friend, not mad; but newly sane.

Come, my victim, come; assist me up

The pillory, there let us stand together—

The woman of The Scarlet Letter,

And he who did this wrong.

First Citizen. That holy man is mad. He an adulterer!

I'll believe it when th' Devil grows blind.

Dimsdell. Support me, Hester.

Dimsdell and Hester ascend pillory together.

Ho! all ye people of the Commonwealth,

Behold the man for whom you oft have sought,

The man who should have borne The Scarlet Letter;

For I am he.

If that the last words of one sinful man

May warn a multitude from sin, who knows

But that his errors tend toward good at last.

Let me not think my suffering in vain,

Or that my crime confessed will lead on others

Unto their downfall.

Behold me as I am—O, what a pang

[*He clutches his breast from now on.*

Was that—a hypocritical adulterer.

Oh!—aye, a base, a low adulterer!

O, God, prolong my breath for this confession!—

I wronged this woman who did fondly love me,

I did neglect her in my cowardice,

I shunned the public scorn.—

O, but a little while!—I stood not with her;

I was a coward; and did deny my child.

Delay! Delay!

Now I avow my crime, I do confess it,

[Kneels] And here I beg you friends, as I have begged

My God, forgive me. Oh, I must be brief—

If any think that while I walked these streets

In seeming honor I lacked my punishment,

Look here.—

[*Tearing shirt open and disclosing stigma.*

O—h!

This cancer did begin to gnaw my breast

When Hester first put on The Scarlet Letter

And never since hath once abated.

Voices. O, wonderful! wonderful! He faints! Help! Help!

Hester. Arthur! Arthur! one word for me! Only one!

Dimsdell. I must say more.

[*Falls.*

Hester. Forgive him, Father! O, God, have mercy now;

Give him but breath to speak to me!

Arthur! Arthur!

Dimsdell. Hester, my Hester, forgive—

[*Dies.*

Hester. Farewell, farewell—dead, dead!

Nay, you shall not take him from me!

My breast shall be his pillow; and, that he may

Rest easy, I here cast off your Scarlet Letter.

Governor. Captain, command your men to bear the body.

A solemn march.

THE END.

About Author

Nathaniel Hawthorne (Hathorne; July 4, 1804 – May 19, 1864) was an American novelist, dark romantic, and short story writer. His works often focus on history, morality, and religion.

He was born in 1804 in Salem, Massachusetts, to Nathaniel Hathorne and the former Elizabeth Clarke Manning. His ancestors include John Hathorne, the only judge involved in the Salem witch trials who never repented of his actions. He entered Bowdoin College in 1821, was elected to Phi Beta Kappa in 1824, and graduated in 1825. He published his first work in 1828, the novel Fanshawe; he later tried to suppress it, feeling that it was not equal to the standard of his later work. He published several short stories in periodicals, which he collected in 1837 as Twice-Told Tales. The next year, he became engaged to Sophia Peabody. He worked at the Boston Custom House and joined Brook Farm, a transcendentalist community, before marrying Peabody in 1842. The couple moved to The Old Manse in Concord, Massachusetts, later moving to Salem, the Berkshires, then to The Wayside in Concord. The Scarlet Letter was published in 1850, followed by a succession of other novels. A political appointment as consul took Hawthorne and family to Europe before their return to Concord in 1860. Hawthorne died on May 19, 1864, and was survived by his wife and their three children.

Much of Hawthorne's writing centers on New England, many works featuring moral metaphors with an anti-Puritan inspiration. His fiction works are considered part of the Romantic movement and, more specifically, dark romanticism. His themes often center on the inherent evil and sin of humanity, and his works often have moral messages and deep psychological complexity. His published works include novels, short stories, and a biography of his college friend Franklin Pierce, the 14th President of the United States.

Biography

Early life

Nathaniel Hawthorne was born on July 4, 1804, in Salem, Massachusetts;

his birthplace is preserved and open to the public. William Hathorne was the author's great-great-great-grandfather. He was a Puritan and was the first of the family to emigrate from England, settling in Dorchester, Massachusetts, before moving to Salem. There he became an important member of the Massachusetts Bay Colony and held many political positions, including magistrate and judge, becoming infamous for his harsh sentencing. William's son and the author's great-great-grandfather John Hathorne was one of the judges who oversaw the Salem witch trials. Hawthorne probably added the "w" to his surname in his early twenties, shortly after graduating from college, in an effort to dissociate himself from his notorious forebears. Hawthorne's father Nathaniel Hathorne Sr. was a sea captain who died in 1808 of yellow fever in Suriname; he had been a member of the East India Marine Society. After his death, his widow moved with young Nathaniel and two daughters to live with relatives named the Mannings in Salem, where they lived for 10 years. Young Hawthorne was hit on the leg while playing "bat and ball" on November 10, 1813, and he became lame and bedridden for a year, though several physicians could find nothing wrong with him.

In the summer of 1816, the family lived as boarders with farmers before moving to a home recently built specifically for them by Hawthorne's uncles Richard and Robert Manning in Raymond, Maine, near Sebago Lake. Years later, Hawthorne looked back at his time in Maine fondly: "Those were delightful days, for that part of the country was wild then, with only scattered clearings, and nine tenths of it primeval woods." In 1819, he was sent back to Salem for school and soon complained of homesickness and being too far from his mother and sisters. He distributed seven issues of The Spectator to his family in August and September 1820 for the sake of having fun. The homemade newspaper was written by hand and included essays, poems, and news featuring the young author's adolescent humor.

Hawthorne's uncle Robert Manning insisted that the boy attend college, despite Hawthorne's protests. With the financial support of his uncle, Hawthorne was sent to Bowdoin College in 1821, partly because of family connections in the area, and also because of its relatively inexpensive tuition rate. Hawthorne met future president Franklin Pierce on the way to

Bowdoin, at the stage stop in Portland, and the two became fast friends. Once at the school, he also met future poet Henry Wadsworth Longfellow, future congressman Jonathan Cilley, and future naval reformer Horatio Bridge. He graduated with the class of 1825, and later described his college experience to Richard Henry Stoddard:

> I was educated (as the phrase is) at Bowdoin College. I was an idle student, negligent of college rules and the Procrustean details of academic life, rather choosing to nurse my own fancies than to dig into Greek roots and be numbered among the learned Thebans.

Early career

In 1836, Hawthorne served as the editor of the American Magazine of Useful and Entertaining Knowledge. At the time, he boarded with poet Thomas Green Fessenden on Hancock Street in Beacon Hill in Boston. He was offered an appointment as weigher and gauger at the Boston Custom House at a salary of $1,500 a year, which he accepted on January 17, 1839. During his time there, he rented a room from George Stillman Hillard, business partner of Charles Sumner. Hawthorne wrote in the comparative obscurity of what he called his "owl's nest" in the family home. As he looked back on this period of his life, he wrote: "I have not lived, but only dreamed about living." He contributed short stories to various magazines and annuals, including "Young Goodman Brown" and "The Minister's Black Veil", though none drew major attention to him. Horatio Bridge offered to cover the risk of collecting these stories in the spring of 1837 into the volume Twice-Told Tales, which made Hawthorne known locally.

Marriage and family

While at Bowdoin, Hawthorne wagered a bottle of Madeira wine with his friend Jonathan Cilley that Cilley would get married before Hawthorne did. By 1836, he had won the bet, but he did not remain a bachelor for life. He had public flirtations with Mary Silsbee and Elizabeth Peabody, then he began pursuing Peabody's sister, illustrator and transcendentalist Sophia Peabody. He joined the transcendentalist Utopian community at Brook Farm in 1841, not because he agreed with the experiment but because it helped him save money to marry Sophia. He paid a $1,000 deposit and was put in charge of shoveling the hill of manure referred to as "the Gold Mine". He left later that year, though his Brook Farm adventure became an inspiration for his novel The Blithedale Romance. Hawthorne married Sophia Peabody on July 9, 1842, at a ceremony in the Peabody parlor on West Street in Boston. The couple moved to The Old Manse in Concord, Massachusetts, where they lived for three years. His neighbor Ralph Waldo Emerson invited him into his social circle, but Hawthorne was almost pathologically shy and stayed silent at gatherings. At the Old Manse, Hawthorne wrote most of the tales collected in Mosses from an Old Manse.

Like Hawthorne, Sophia was a reclusive person. Throughout her early life, she had frequent migraines and underwent several experimental medical treatments. She was mostly bedridden until her sister introduced her to Hawthorne, after which her headaches seem to have abated. The Hawthornes enjoyed a long and happy marriage. He referred to her as his "Dove" and wrote that she "is, in the strictest sense, my sole companion; and I need no other—there is no vacancy in my mind, any more than in my heart ... Thank God that I suffice for her boundless heart!" Sophia greatly admired her husband's work. She wrote in one of her journals:

> I am always so dazzled and bewildered with the richness, the depth, the ... jewels of beauty in his productions that I am always looking forward to a second reading where I can ponder and muse and fully take in the miraculous wealth of thoughts.

Poet Ellery Channing came to the Old Manse for help on the first anniversary of the Hawthornes' marriage. A local teenager named Martha Hunt had drowned herself in the river and Hawthorne's boat Pond Lily was needed to find her body. Hawthorne helped recover the corpse, which he described as "a spectacle of such perfect horror ... She was the very image of death-agony". The incident later inspired a scene in his novel The Blithedale Romance.

The Hawthornes had three children. Their first was daughter Una, born March 3, 1844; her name was a reference to The Faerie Queene, to the displeasure of family members. Hawthorne wrote to a friend, "I find it a very sober and serious kind of happiness that springs from the birth of a child ... There is no escaping it any longer. I have business on earth now, and must look about me for the means of doing it." In October 1845, the Hawthornes moved to Salem. In 1846, their son Julian was born. Hawthorne wrote to his sister Louisa on June 22, 1846: "A small troglodyte made his appearance here at ten minutes to six o'clock this morning, who claimed to be your nephew." Daughter Rose was born in May 1851, and Hawthorne called her his "autumnal flower".

Middle years

In April 1846, Hawthorne was officially appointed the Surveyor for the District of Salem and Beverly and Inspector of the Revenue for the Port of Salem at an annual salary of $1,200. He had difficulty writing during this period, as he admitted to Longfellow:

> I am trying to resume my pen ... Whenever I sit alone, or walk alone, I find myself dreaming about stories, as of old; but these forenoons in the Custom House undo all that the afternoons and evenings have done. I should be happier if I could write.

This employment, like his earlier appointment to the custom house in Boston, was vulnerable to the politics of the spoils system. Hawthorne was a Democrat and lost this job due to the change of administration in Washington after the presidential election of 1848. He wrote a letter of protest to the Boston Daily Advertiser which was attacked by the Whigs and supported by the Democrats, making Hawthorne's dismissal a much-talked about event in New England. He was deeply affected by the death of his mother in late July, calling it "the darkest hour I ever lived". He was appointed the corresponding secretary of the Salem Lyceum in 1848. Guests who came to speak that season included Emerson, Thoreau, Louis Agassiz, and Theodore Parker.

Hawthorne returned to writing and published The Scarlet Letter in mid-March 1850, including a preface that refers to his three-year tenure in the Custom House and makes several allusions to local politicians—who did not appreciate their treatment. It was one of the first mass-produced books in America, selling 2,500 volumes within ten days and earning Hawthorne $1,500 over 14 years. The book was pirated by booksellers in London and became a best-seller in the United States; it initiated his most lucrative period as a writer. Hawthorne's friend Edwin Percy Whipple objected to the novel's "morbid intensity" and its dense psychological details, writing that the book "is therefore apt to become, like Hawthorne, too painfully anatomical in his exhibition of them", though 20th-century writer D. H. Lawrence said that there could be no more perfect work of the American imagination than The Scarlet Letter.

Hawthorne and his family moved to a small red farmhouse near Lenox, Massachusetts, at the end of March 1850. He became friends with Herman Melville beginning on August 5, 1850, when the authors met at a picnic hosted by a mutual friend. Melville had just read Hawthorne's short story collection Mosses from an Old Manse, and his unsigned review of the collection was printed in The Literary World on August 17 and August 24 titled "Hawthorne and His Mosses". Melville wrote that these stories revealed a dark side to Hawthorne, "shrouded in blackness, ten times black". He was composing his novel Moby-Dick at the time, and dedicated the work in 1851 to Hawthorne: "In token of my admiration for his genius, this book is inscribed to Nathaniel Hawthorne."

Hawthorne's time in the Berkshires was very productive. While there, he wrote The House of the Seven Gables (1851), which poet and critic James Russell Lowell said was better than The Scarlet Letter and called "the most valuable contribution to New England history that has been made." He also wrote The Blithedale Romance (1852), his only work written in the first person. He also published A Wonder-Book for Girls and Boys in 1851, a collection of short stories retelling myths which he had been thinking about writing since 1846. Nevertheless, poet Ellery Channing reported that Hawthorne "has suffered much living in this place". The family enjoyed the scenery of the Berkshires, although Hawthorne did not enjoy the winters in their small house. They left on November 21, 1851. Hawthorne noted, "I am sick to death of Berkshire ... I have felt languid and dispirited, during almost my whole residence."

The Wayside and Europe

In May 1852, the Hawthornes returned to Concord where they lived until July 1853. In February, they bought The Hillside, a home previously inhabited by Amos Bronson Alcott and his family, and renamed it The Wayside. Their neighbors in Concord included Emerson and Henry David Thoreau. That year, Hawthorne wrote The Life of Franklin Pierce, the campaign biography of his friend which depicted him as "a man of peaceful pursuits". Horace Mann said, "If he makes out Pierce to be a great man or a brave man, it will be the greatest work of fiction he ever wrote." In the biography, Hawthorne depicts Pierce as a statesman and soldier who had accomplished no great feats because of his need to make "little noise" and so "withdrew into the background". He also left out Pierce's drinking habits, despite rumors of his alcoholism, and emphasized Pierce's belief that slavery could not "be remedied by human contrivances" but would, over time, "vanish like a dream".

With Pierce's election as President, Hawthorne was rewarded in 1853 with the position of United States consul in Liverpool shortly after the publication of Tanglewood Tales. The role was considered the most lucrative foreign service position at the time, described by Hawthorne's wife as "second in dignity to the Embassy in London". His appointment ended in 1857 at the close of the Pierce administration, and the Hawthorne family toured France and Italy. During his time in Italy, the previously clean-shaven Hawthorne grew a bushy mustache.

The family returned to The Wayside in 1860, and that year saw the publication of The Marble Faun, his first new book in seven years. Hawthorne admitted that he had aged considerably, referring to himself as "wrinkled with time and trouble".

Later years and death

At the outset of the American Civil War, Hawthorne traveled with William D. Ticknor to Washington, D.C., where he met Abraham Lincoln and other notable figures. He wrote about his experiences in the essay "Chiefly About War Matters" in 1862.

Failing health prevented him from completing several more romance novels. Hawthorne was suffering from pain in his stomach and insisted on a recuperative trip with his friend Franklin Pierce, though his neighbor Bronson Alcott was concerned that Hawthorne was too ill. While on a tour of the White Mountains, he died in his sleep on May 19, 1864, in Plymouth, New Hampshire. Pierce sent a telegram to Elizabeth Peabody asking her to inform Mrs. Hawthorne in person. Mrs. Hawthorne was too saddened by the news to handle the funeral arrangements herself. Hawthorne's son Julian was a freshman at Harvard College, and he learned of his father's death the next day; coincidentally, he was initiated into the Delta Kappa Epsilon fraternity on the same day by being blindfolded and placed in a coffin.Longfellow wrote a tribute poem to Hawthorne published in 1866 called "The Bells of Lynn". Hawthorne was buried on what is now known as "Authors' Ridge" in Sleepy Hollow Cemetery, Concord, Massachusetts. Pallbearers included Longfellow, Emerson, Alcott, Oliver Wendell Holmes Sr., James Thomas Fields, and Edwin Percy Whipple. Emerson wrote of the funeral: "I thought there was a tragic element in the event, that might be more fully rendered—in the painful solitude of the man, which, I suppose, could no longer be endured, & he died of it."

His wife Sophia and daughter Una were originally buried in England. However, in June 2006, they were reinterred in plots adjacent to Hawthorne.

Writings

Hawthorne had a particularly close relationship with his publishers William Ticknor and James Thomas Fields. Hawthorne once told Fields, "I care more for your good opinion than for that of a host of critics." In fact, it was Fields who convinced Hawthorne to turn The Scarlet Letter into a novel rather than a short story. Ticknor handled many of Hawthorne's personal matters, including the purchase of cigars, overseeing financial accounts, and even purchasing clothes. Ticknor died with Hawthorne at his side in Philadelphia in 1864; according to a friend, Hawthorne was left "apparently dazed".

Literary style and themes

Hawthorne's works belong to romanticism or, more specifically, dark romanticism, cautionary tales that suggest that guilt, sin, and evil are the most inherent natural qualities of humanity. Many of his works are inspired by Puritan New England, combining historical romance loaded with symbolism and deep psychological themes, bordering on surrealism. His depictions of the past are a version of historical fiction used only as a vehicle to express common themes of ancestral sin, guilt and retribution. His later writings also reflect his negative view of the Transcendentalism movement.

Hawthorne was predominantly a short story writer in his early career. Upon publishing Twice-Told Tales, however, he noted, "I do not think much of them," and he expected little response from the public. His four major romances were written between 1850 and 1860: The Scarlet Letter (1850), The House of the Seven Gables (1851), The Blithedale Romance (1852) and The Marble Faun (1860). Another novel-length romance, Fanshawe, was published anonymously in 1828. Hawthorne defined a romance as being radically different from a novel by not being concerned with the possible or probable course of ordinary experience. In the preface to The House of the Seven Gables, Hawthorne describes his romance-writing as using "atmospherical medium as to bring out or mellow the lights and deepen and enrich the shadows of the picture". The picture, Daniel Hoffman found, was one of "the primitive energies of fecundity and creation."

Critics have applied feminist perspectives and historicist approaches to Hawthorne's depictions of women. Feminist scholars are interested particularly in Hester Prynne: they recognize that while she herself could not be the "destined prophetess" of the future, the "angel and apostle of the coming revelation" must nevertheless "be a woman." Camille Paglia saw Hester as mystical, "a wandering goddess still bearing the mark of her Asiatic origins ... moving serenely in the magic circle of her sexual nature". Lauren Berlant termed Hester "the citizen as woman [personifying] love as a quality of the body that contains the purest light of nature," her resulting "traitorous political theory" a "Female Symbolic" literalization of futile Puritan metaphors. Historicists view Hester as a protofeminist and avatar of the self-reliance and responsibility that led to women's suffrage and reproductive emancipation. Anthony Splendora found her literary genealogy among other archetypally fallen but redeemed women, both historic and mythic. As examples, he offers Psyche of ancient legend; Heloise of twelfth-century France's tragedy involving world-renowned philosopher Peter Abelard; Anne Hutchinson (America's first heretic, circa 1636), and Hawthorne family friend Margaret Fuller. In Hester's first appearance, Hawthorne likens her, "infant at her bosom", to Mary, Mother of Jesus, "the image of Divine Maternity". In her study of Victorian literature, in which such "galvanic outcasts" as Hester feature prominently, Nina Auerbach went so far as to name Hester's fall and subsequent redemption, "the novel's one unequivocally religious activity". Regarding Hester as a deity figure, Meredith A. Powers found in Hester's characterization "the earliest in American fiction that the archetypal Goddess appears quite graphically," like a Goddess "not the wife of traditional marriage, permanently subject to a male overlord"; Powers noted "her syncretism, her flexibility, her inherent ability to alter and so avoid the defeat of secondary status in a goal-oriented civilization".

Aside from Hester Prynne, the model women of Hawthorne's other novels—from Ellen Langton of Fanshawe to Zenobia and Priscilla of The Blithedale Romance, Hilda and Miriam of The Marble Faun and Phoebe and Hepzibah of The House of the Seven Gables—are more fully realized than his male characters, who merely orbit them. This observation is equally true of his short-stories, in which central females serve as allegorical figures: Rappaccini's beautiful but life-altering, garden-bound, daughter; almost-perfect Georgiana of "The Birthmark"; the sinned-against (abandoned) Ester of "Ethan Brand"; and goodwife Faith Brown, linchpin of Young Goodman Brown's very belief in God. "My Faith is gone!" Brown exclaims in despair upon seeing his wife at the Witches' Sabbath. Perhaps the most sweeping statement of Hawthorne's impetus comes from Mark Van Doren: "Somewhere, if not in the New England of his time, Hawthorne unearthed the image of a goddess supreme in beauty and power."

Hawthorne also wrote nonfiction. In 2008, the Library of America selected Hawthorne's "A show of wax-figures" for inclusion in its two-century retrospective of American True Crime.

Criticism

In "Hawthorne and His Mosses", Herman Melville wrote a passionate argument for Hawthorne to be among the burgeoning American literary canon, "He is one of the new, and far better generation of your writers." In this review of Mosses from an Old Manse, Melville describes an affinity for Hawthorne that would only increase: "I feel that this Hawthorne has dropped germinous seeds into my soul. He expands and deepens down, the more I contemplate him; and further, and further, shoots his strong New-England roots into the hot soil of my Southern soul." Edgar Allan Poe wrote important reviews of both Twice-Told Tales and Mosses from an Old Manse. Poe's assessment was partly informed by his contempt of allegory and moral tales, and his chronic accusations of plagiarism, though he admitted,

> The style of Mr. Hawthorne is purity itself. His tone is singularly effective—wild, plaintive, thoughtful, and in full accordance with his themes ... We look upon him as one of the few men of indisputable genius to whom our country has as yet given birth.

Ralph Waldo Emerson wrote, "Nathaniel Hawthorne's reputation as a writer is a very pleasing fact, because his writing is not good for anything, and this is a tribute to the man." Henry James praised Hawthorne, saying, "The fine thing in Hawthorne is that he cared for the deeper psychology, and that, in his way, he tried to become familiar with it." Poet John Greenleaf Whittier wrote that he admired the "weird and subtle beauty" in Hawthorne's tales. Evert Augustus Duyckinck said of Hawthorne, "Of the American writers destined to live, he is the most original, the one least indebted to foreign models or literary precedents of any kind."

Contemporary response to Hawthorne's work praised his sentimentality and moral purity while more modern evaluations focus on the dark psychological complexity. Beginning in the 1950s, critics have focused on symbolism and didacticism.

The critic Harold Bloom opined that only Henry James and William Faulkner challenge Hawthorne's position as the greatest American novelist, although he admitted that he favored James as the greatest American novelist.

Bloom saw Hawthorne's greatest works to be principally The Scarlet Letter, followed by The Marble Faun and certain short stories, including "My Kinsman, Major Molineux", "Young Goodman Brown", "Wakefield", and "Feathertop". (Source: Wikipedia)

NOTABLE WORKS

NOVELS

Fanshawe (published anonymously, 1828)

The Scarlet Letter (1850)

The House of the Seven Gables (1851)

The Blithedale Romance (1852)

The Marble Faun: Or, The Romance of Monte Beni (1860) (as Transformation: Or, The Romance of Monte Beni, UK publication, same year)

The Dolliver Romance (1863) (unfinished)

Septimius Felton; or, the Elixir of Life (unfinished, published in the Atlantic Monthly, 1872)

Doctor Grimshawe's Secret: A Romance (unfinished, with preface and notes by Julian Hawthorne, 1882)

SHORT STORY COLLECTIONS

Twice-Told Tales (1837)

Grandfather's Chair (1840)

Mosses from an Old Manse (1846)

A Wonder-Book for Girls and Boys (1851)

The Snow-Image, and Other Twice-Told Tales (1852)

Tanglewood Tales (1853)

The Dolliver Romance and Other Pieces (1876)

The Great Stone Face and Other Tales of the White Mountains (1889)

SELECTED SHORT STORIES

"The Hollow of the Three Hills" (1830)

"Roger Malvin's Burial" (1832)

"My Kinsman, Major Molineux" (1832)

"The Minister's Black Veil" (1832)

"Young Goodman Brown" (1835)

"The Gray Champion" (1835)

"The White Old Maid" (1835)

"Wakefield" (1835)

"The Ambitious Guest" (1835)

"The Man of Adamant" (1837)

"The May-Pole of Merry Mount" (1837)

"The Great Carbuncle" (1837)

"Dr. Heidegger's Experiment" (1837)

"A Virtuoso's Collection" (May 1842)

"The Birth-Mark" (March 1843)

"The Celestial Railroad" (1843)

"Egotism; or, The Bosom-Serpent" (1843)

"Earth's Holocaust" (1844)

"Rappaccini's Daughter" (1844)

"P.'s Correspondence" (1845)

"The Artist of the Beautiful" (1846)

"Fire Worship" (1846)

"Ethan Brand" (1850)

"The Great Stone Face" (1850)

"Feathertop" (1852)

NONFICTION

Twenty Days with Julian & Little Bunny (written 1851, published 1904)

Our Old Home (1863)

Passages from the French and Italian Notebooks (1871)

CPSIA information can be obtained
at www.ICGtesting.com
Printed in the USA
LVHW092018130720
660559LV00005B/462